Cambridge Elements ≡

Elements in the Philosophy of Biology
edited by
Grant Ramsey
KU Leuven
Michael Ruse
Florida State University

SOCIAL DARWINISM

Jeffrey O'Connell
Florida State University
Michael Ruse
Florida State University

CAMBRIDGE
UNIVERSITY PRESS

CAMBRIDGE
UNIVERSITY PRESS

University Printing House, Cambridge CB2 8BS, United Kingdom

One Liberty Plaza, 20th Floor, New York, NY 10006, USA

477 Williamstown Road, Port Melbourne, VIC 3207, Australia

314–321, 3rd Floor, Plot 3, Splendor Forum, Jasola District Centre, New Delhi – 110025, India

79 Anson Road, #06–04/06, Singapore 079906

Cambridge University Press is part of the University of Cambridge.

It furthers the University's mission by disseminating knowledge in the pursuit of education, learning, and research at the highest international levels of excellence.

www.cambridge.org
Information on this title: www.cambridge.org/9781108793803
DOI: 10.1017/9781108879026

© Jeffrey O'Connell and Michael Ruse 2021

First published 2021

A catalogue record for this publication is available from the British Library.

ISBN 978-1-108-79380-3 Paperback
ISSN 2515-1126 (online)
ISSN 2515-1118 (print)

Cambridge University Press has no responsibility for the persistence or accuracy of URLs for external or third-party internet websites referred to in this publication and does not guarantee that any content on such websites is, or will remain, accurate or appropriate.

Social Darwinism

Elements in the Philosophy of Biology

DOI: 10.1017/9781108879026
First published online: May 2021

Jeffrey O'Connell
Florida State University

Michael Ruse
Florida State University

Author for correspondence: Michael Ruse - mruse@fsu.edu, Jeffrey O'Connell - jeff.m.oconnell@gmail.com

Abstract: This Element is a philosophical history of Social Darwinism. It begins by discussing the meaning of the term, moving then to its origins, paying particular attention to whether it is Charles Darwin or Herbert Spencer who is the true father of the idea. It gives an exposition of early thinking on the subject, covering Darwin and Spencer themselves, and then on to Social Darwinism as found in American thought, with special emphasis on Andrew Carnegie, and Germany with special emphasis on Friedrich von Bernhardi. Attention is also paid to outliers, notably the Englishman Alfred Russel Wallace, the Russian Peter Kropotkin, and the German Friedrich Nietzsche. From here we move into the twentieth century, looking at Adolf Hitler – hardly a regular Social Darwinian given he did not believe in evolution – and in the Anglophone world, Julian Huxley and Edward O. Wilson, who reflected the concerns of their society.

Keywords: Charles Darwin, Social Darwinism, Herbert Spencer, Andrew Carnegie, Friedrich Nietzsche

ISBNs: 9781108793803 (PB), 9781108879026 (OC)
ISSNs: 2515-1126 (online), 2515-1118 (print)

Contents

1 Introduction

In 1877, in an extremely technical discussion of landholding in Ireland, Joseph Fisher wrote: "I can find nothing in the Brehon laws to warrant this theory of social Darwinism, and believe further study will show that the Cain Saerrath and the Cain Aigillue relate solely to what we now call chattels, and did not in any way affect what we now call the freehold, the possession of the land" (Fisher 1877). "Cain Saerrath" refers to laws to do with honor and personal relationships and "Cain Aigillue" to laws to do with forfeits and fines. Fisher is arguing that the holding of large tracts of land by individuals is unwarranted in traditional law. It seems that he himself made up the term "social Darwinism." Although there may not have been precedent, obviously he has Darwin's theory in mind, especially the thoughts about the struggle for existence. What is not at all obvious is that he thinks of "social Darwinism" as an item, a single identifiable concept, as opposed to Darwinism in a social situation. What we can say is that, for all that he himself is using the language of "social Darwinism" in a negative sort of way, there is no justification for the claim (nor is it being made) that social Darwinism – meaning digging out the ethical implications of evolutionary theorizing and applying them to society – is always something negative (Leonard 2009).

As the term started to be used more and more often, so in tandem its bad reputation rose, to the extent that no one wanted to be thought a social Darwinian – that was a term used of opponents! And so to social Darwinism's reputation today. Google it! "The concept of Social Darwinism attempted to justify and rationalize ideas of imperialism, hereditarianism and racism." That's before you get to big business. "The theory of Social Darwinism was used to support Free Enterprise and 'laissez-faire' capitalism combined with political conservatism during the Gilded Era." And widows and children? Tough luck. "The belief that it was not the function of the Government to cure social problems." It is a safe bet that in discussions like these the name of Adolf Hitler will come up, probably sooner rather than later. You would not be wrong. "The most infamous instance of Social Darwinism in action is in the genocidal policies of the Nazi German Government in the 1930s and 40s. It was openly embraced as promoting the notion that the strongest should naturally prevail, and was a key feature of Nazi propaganda films, some which illustrated it with scenes of beetles fighting each other."[1]

"Beetles fighting each other"?! When ideas have this kind of reputation and supposed inclinations, scholars sense red meat. To say that the topic of social Darwinism is a field well-ploughed is a bit like saying that parallel lines never

---

[1] www.historyhit.com/social-darwinism-in-nazi-germany/

meet. The literature is huge.[2] Why then yet more? Our justification for turning to this topic is that, rather than as historians and folk from other fields, who have dominated the discussion, we write as philosophers. We think there are issues of importance for people like us. Be warned, however, that because we are philosophers our underlying intent and hope is to ferret out truths about human beings. You may fear that this means our turning to history is part of what is known as a "Whiggish" agenda, where we are simply using the past to burnish the better, much-improved present. Far from it! We are evolutionists and we believe that, in order to understand the present, you need to understand the past. Exploring conceptual foundations, we start with Darwin himself and the implications of his theorizing for moral understanding. It is only then that we move to the subsequent history, but still with philosophical intent. Darwinian evolutionary theory is generally considered the jewel in the crown of biology, if not of modern science overall. How then could it have transmogrified and degenerated to such an awful form? From Charles Darwin, the quintessential Victorian gentleman, to Adolf Hitler, the quintessential twentieth-century tyrant? And within less than a century. Darwin's *Origin of Species* appeared in 1859. Hitler's *Mein Kampf* in 1925. A mere sixty-six years. What does this tell us about the nature of science? Copernicus did not lead to the gas chambers. Is there something peculiar about Darwin's theory? Is it perhaps not really a scientific theory at all? And what are the implications for today?

These are the sorts of questions we raise. Questions that presuppose historical understanding but are not quite historical themselves. As is so often the case in these sorts of things, it turns out that the full story is very much more complex – and more interesting – than the popular account referred to just above. This is the real justification of this Element. Begin with Darwin's theory.[3]

---

[2] The classic discussion is Richard Hofstadter, 1959. *Social Darwinism in American Thought*. Robert Bannister, *Social Darwinism: Science and Myth in Anglo-American Social Thought* is the revisionist account challenging every one of Hofstadter's claims, including the one that there is such a concept as social Darwinism! Indispensable, although lengthy and turgid as only academics know how, is D. C. Bellomy, 1984. "Social Darwinism revisited," *Perspectives in American History, New Series, 1984*. Also valuable are Greta Jones, 1980, *Social Darwinism and English Thought,* and Mike Hawkins, 1997, *Social Darwinism in European and American Thought, 1860–1945.* For those hesitant to plunge right into such turbulent seas, Gregory Radick, "Darwinism and Social Darwinism" (2018) offers an excellent wading pool for beginners.

[3] Because an Element is an extended essay rather than a full-length monograph, intentionally we have stayed on topic, avoiding discussion of related issues like eugenics. Also, we have confined the discussion to Britain, America, and Germany, leaving social Darwinism elsewhere, as in Asia and South America, unexplored. Parts of this Element draw on previous writings by the authors, most particularly the co-authored "After Darwin: morality in a secular world," from *Secular Studies* (2019). Everything is used with permission.

2 Charles Darwin's Theory of Evolution

Charles Robert Darwin was born in England on February 12, 1809, the same day as Abraham Lincoln across the Atlantic. He died, also in England, on April 19, 1882, and was buried in Westminster Abbey, next to the great physicist Isaac Newton (Browne 1995, 2002). His family was distinguished and rich. His paternal grandfather, Erasmus Darwin, had been a physician, poet, and early evolutionist. His maternal grandfather, Josiah Wedgwood, was the founder of the pottery works that still carries his name. Rather deliberately keeping the fortune within the family, Darwin married his first cousin Emma Wedgwood, also a grandchild of the first Josiah Wedgwood. Charles Darwin never had to work for a living. After education at Edinburgh and Cambridge, Darwin became a full-time scientist – first geologist and then biologist. No one ever doubted that he was a professional.

Following Cambridge, Darwin spent five years (1831–6) going around the globe on the British warship HMS *Beagle*. The navy was mapping the coastlines of countries that were, or had the potential to be, commercial markets. Darwin spent most of his time crisscrossing South America. He kept a diary, which he wrote up as a very popular travel book – *The Voyage of the Beagle*. On his return to England, Darwin soon became an evolutionist – primarily because of the distribution of the organisms on the Galapagos archipelago (in the Pacific, today belonging to Ecuador). Then, eighteen months later, Darwin discovered his mechanism of natural selection. He wrote up preliminary versions of his theory in 1842 and 1844, but kept them private, probably because he did not want to upset his powerful scientific mentors. He fell sick. The cause may have been lactose intolerance. Finally, in 1859, thanks to the arrival of an essay mirroring his ideas by the young naturalist Alfred Russel Wallace, Darwin published *On the Origin of Species by Means of Natural Selection, or the Preservation of Favored Races in the Struggle for Life*. The work was influential and controversial. More on this in a minute. Darwin left most of the defense of his thinking to his younger colleagues and supporters, notably the morphologist and paleontologist, and notable essayist, Thomas Henry Huxley. What Darwin did do, spurred primarily by the apostasy of Wallace, who started arguing that human evolution was fueled by spirit forces, was write a follow-up book on our species, *The Descent of Man, and Selection in Relation to Sex* (1871).

The *Origin* is written in a deceptively simple, "user-friendly" way. In fact, it is one long, very carefully constructed argument (Ruse 1979a). Darwin starts with the analogy between artificial selection – that process practiced by breeders – and natural selection – what he presumes happens in the real world. Farmers breed fatter pigs, stronger horses, better milk-producing cows.

Fanciers and sportsmen breed more songful canaries and tougher dogs. Given the tremendous changes they produce, why not something similar in nature? Then Darwin moves to the central case for natural selection. This is two-part. First there is the argument to the struggle for existence. Expounded first by the eighteenth-century clergyman/political scientist Thomas Robert Malthus, this is something that comes about because the potential for reproduction much outstrips the availability of food and space. "Every being, which during its natural lifetime produces several eggs or seeds, must suffer destruction during some period of its life, and during some season or occasional year, otherwise, on the principle of geometrical increase, its numbers would quickly become so inordinately great that no country could support the product." The conclusion follows at once: "as more individuals are produced than can possibly survive, there must in every case be a struggle for existence, either one individual with another of the same species, or with the individuals of distinct species, or with the physical conditions of life" (Darwin 1859, 63–64). Then, drawing on the fact that, whenever you have a population of organisms, you find that there are differences between them and that, every now and then, something new seems to pop up into being – new variations – there is the argument to natural selection. If there are such variations, "can we doubt (remembering that many more individuals are born than can possibly survive) that individuals having any advantage, however slight, over others, would have the best chance of surviving and of procreating their kind? On the other hand, we may feel sure that any variation in the least degree injurious would be rigidly destroyed. This preservation of favourable variations and the rejection of injurious variations, I call Natural Selection" (80–81).

Do note that, for Darwin, change was not random. Certain features lead to success. Others do not. This means that the successful features have virtues not possessed by the unsuccessful. All in all, this means that features like the hand and the eye are "as if" designed for their ends – they are "adaptations." "How have all those exquisite adaptations of one part of the organisation to another part, and to the conditions of life, and of one distinct organic being to another being, been perfected? We see these beautiful coadaptations most plainly in the woodpecker and missletoe; and only a little less plainly in the humblest parasite which clings to the hairs of a quadruped or feathers of a bird; in the structure of the beetle which dives through the water; in the plumed seed which is wafted by the gentlest breeze; in short, we see beautiful adaptations everywhere and in every part of the organic world" (60–61).

Guided by the analogy with artificial selection, where one has two classes of end – for utility, as with farm breeders, and for beauty and fighting spirit, as with fanciers and sportsmen – Darwin added a secondary mechanism of sexual selection. Where natural selection is for adaptations that help organisms survive, sexual selection is for adaptations that help organisms find mates. And now, with selection introduced, Darwin added some complexifying factors, most particularly the division of labor (or "labour" as he writes it). Organisms specialize, as do workers in a factory. "So in the general economy of any land, the more widely and perfectly the animals and plants are diversified for different habits of life, so will a greater number of individuals be capable of their supporting themselves. A set of animals, with their organisation but little diversified, could hardly compete with a set more perfectly diversified in structure" (116). And so to the famous metaphor of a tree of life. "The affinities of all the beings of the same class have sometimes been represented by a great tree. I believe this simile largely speaks the truth." Continuing: "As buds give rise by growth to fresh buds, and these, if vigorous, branch out and overtop on all sides many a feebler branch, so by generation I believe it has been with the great Tree of Life, which fills with its dead and broken branches the crust of the earth, and covers the surface with its ever branching and beautiful ramifications" (130).

The second half of the *Origin* applies this causal thinking to a wide range of problems across the whole of the life sciences. Invoking what the philosopher of science William Whewell (1840) called a "consilience of inductions," Darwin explained and at the same time supported. As evolution through selection explains, for instance, why the birds of the Galapagos look like the birds of South America and why the birds of the Canaries look like the birds of Africa – descendants on the islands came from the respective continents, and when there evolved further – so these facts of biogeography confirm the reality and power of selection. The detective's hypothesis explains the bloodstains, and, at the same time, the bloodstains confirm the truth of the hypothesis. Social behavior, paleontology, biogeography, morphology, systematics and embryology were taken out, dusted and returned cleaner. Less metaphorically, these various disciplines were illuminated by selection and, in turn, confirmed its power and worth.

And so finally to the most famous passage in the history of science.

> It is interesting to contemplate an entangled bank, clothed with many plants of many kinds, with birds singing on the bushes, with various insects flitting about, and with worms crawling through the damp earth, and to reflect that these elaborately constructed forms, so different from each other, and dependent on each other in so complex a manner, have all been produced by laws acting around us. These laws, taken in the largest sense, being Growth with Reproduction; Inheritance which is almost implied by reproduction; Variability from the indirect and direct action of the external

conditions of life, and from use and disuse; a Ratio of Increase so high as to lead to a Struggle for Life, and as a consequence to Natural Selection, entailing Divergence of Character and the Extinction of less-improved forms. Thus, from the war of nature, from famine and death, the most exalted object which we are capable of conceiving, namely, the production of the higher animals, directly follows. There is grandeur in this view of life, with its several powers, having been originally breathed into a few forms or into one; and that, whilst this planet has gone cycling on according to the fixed law of gravity, from so simple a beginning endless forms most beautiful and most wonderful have been, and are being, evolved. (489–490)

What about our own species, *Homo sapiens*? From the first, Darwin was stone-cold certain that we humans are part of the natural world, produced by the same processes as all other organisms. In his private notebooks of 1839, it is in the human context we find the first unambiguous mention of natural selection. Children, by chance, "produced with strong arms, outliving the weaker ones, may be applicable to the formation of instincts, independently of habits" (Darwin 1987, N 42). Not just humans but our brains and hence our minds! Darwin would have given those much-criticized human sociobiologists of the 1970s – of whom, more later – a good run for their money. However, Darwin knew that, as soon as he published, everyone would be all over the implications of the theory for humankind – as they were, talking at once of the "monkey theory" or likewise. He wanted to get the basic ideas out first. Humans could wait. Hence, so he would not be accused of cowardice, there was right at the end a brief trailer for the human question, but that was it. "In the distant future I see open fields for far more important researches. Psychology will be based on a new foundation, that of the necessary acquirement of each mental power and capacity by gradation. Light will be thrown on the origin of man and his history" (Darwin 1859, 488).

Possibly – probably – for Darwin that would have been his only and final word on the human problem. Wallace's apostasy saw that this could not be, and so twelve years later we got the *Descent of Man*. It is very much written as a follow-up to the *Origin*, although there is much more use of secondary material and more open speculation about value issues. The standard picture is unchanged. Humans are primates and we evolved from the apes – not apes of a kind that exist today, but apes nevertheless. Going a bit against the tide – people were not keen on having "negro" ancestors – Darwin opted for Africa as our place of origin, not the more popular Asia. What was innovative was a very heavy reliance on sexual selection. Wallace had argued that things like intelligence and hairlessness could not have evolved by natural selection and must have had the aid of spirit forces. Rejecting the conclusion but accepting the premises, Darwin argued that such characteristics were produced by sexual selection. The cleverer men got the prize women, and the less hairy males appealed to the better class of female. All this led to some very Victorian conclusions. He-men. "Man is more courageous, pugnacious, and energetic than woman, and has a more inventive genius. His brain is absolutely larger, but whether relatively to the larger size of his body, in comparison with that of woman, has not, I believe been fully ascertained." She-girls. "In woman the face is rounder; the jaws and the base of the skull smaller; the outlines of her body rounder, in parts more prominent; and her pelvis is broader than in man; but this latter character may perhaps be considered rather as a primary than a secondary sexual character. She comes to maturity at an earlier age than man" (Darwin 1871, 2, 316–317). And so on and so forth at very great length.

3 Darwin on Morality

Now we start to move to our focus of interest. By the 1870s, among intellectuals (in Britain and America), God-belief was in a bad way. More and more people, including Darwin himself, inclined to some form of what Thomas Henry Huxley had called "agnosticism." Does God exist? I don't know and I am not terribly worried. Start with science. While on the *Beagle* voyage, Darwin moved from theism, in his case belief in the God of Christianity, to deism, belief in an Unmoved Mover. He moved from a God who is prepared to intervene in His creation to a God who worked through unbroken law. Darwin simply could not reconcile miracles with the beliefs of common sense, including the lawlike nature of the world. Many were starting to think this way, although in respects more important than science was the so-called German "higher criticism," treating the books of the Bible as humanly written rather than directly from on high. Moses, for instance, did not write the first five books of the canon. As soon as one started to think this way, the literal authenticity of all the Bible, including the Gospels, started to crumble, and with it went the God of the Christians.

The very claims of Christianity came under very critical scrutiny. It was here that Darwin parted ways with religious belief. "I can indeed hardly see how anyone ought to wish Christianity to be true; for if so the plain language of the text seems to show that the men who do not believe, and this would include my Father, Brother and almost all my best friends, will be everlastingly punished." Adding: "And this is a damnable doctrine" (Darwin 1958, 87). One adds to this that, sociologically, Christianity was seemingly out of date. It worked as a uniting ideology in the village with the squire and the yokels, but, in the urban world of factories, it seemed outdated and unneeded. That good Christian

Charles Dickens spotted this. In *Hard Times*, with acid tongue in cheek, he wrote of the churches of Coketown, the industrial city in which his story occurs, that: "The perplexing mystery of the place was, Who belonged to the eighteen denominations? Because, whoever did, the labouring people did not." Walk the streets on a Sunday, "and note how few of them the barbarous jangling of bells that was driving the sick and nervous mad, called away from their own quarter, from their own close rooms, from the corners of their own streets, where they lounged listlessly, gazing at all the church and chapel going, as at a thing with which they had no manner of concern" (Dickens [1854] 1948, 23).

A century before the *Descent*, the Scottish philosopher David Hume had dismissed religious belief as a delusion. "We find human faces in the moon, armies in the clouds; and by a natural propensity, if not corrected by experience and reflection, ascribe malice and good will to everything that hurts or pleases us" (Hume 1757). As a young man, Darwin had read Hume's *History of Religion* from which this line is taken. He took the same tack: "my dog, a full-grown and very sensible animal, was lying on the lawn during a hot and still day; but at a little distance a slight breeze occasionally moved an open parasol, which would have been wholly disregarded by the dog, had any one stood near it. As it was, every time that the parasol slightly moved, the dog growled fiercely and barked. He must, I think, have reasoned to himself in a rapid and unconscious manner, that movement without any apparent cause indicated the presence of some strange living agent, and no stranger had a right to be on his territory" (Darwin 1871, 1, 67). Adding: "The belief in spiritual agencies would easily pass into the belief in the existence of one or more gods."

We come to morality. Let's start with the fact that the last thing wanted by the agnostics was a rejection of right and wrong. George Eliot, the novelist, who as a young woman translated into English the classic of higher criticism, David Strauss's *Life of Jesus*, was obsessive on this topic. Anyone who read her novels, *Daniel Deronda* for instance, with the triumph of the noble title character and the tragedy of the selfish Gwendoline, knew that. After her death, a friend wrote: "I remember how, at Cambridge, I walked with her once in the Fellows' Garden of Trinity, on an evening of rainy May; and she, stirred somewhat beyond her wont, and taking as her text the three words which have been used so often as the inspiring trumpet-calls of men—the words God, Immortality, Duty—pronounced, with terrible earnestness, how inconceivable was the first, how unbelievable the second, and yet how peremptory and absolute the third." (Myers 1881, 47)

Darwin and his followers fit right in here. Darwin and his family lived in the village of Downe, in Kent, where his closest friend was the local Anglican clergyman, John Brodie Innes. Between them they ran the "Coal and Country

Club," designed to help the working class to save for difficult times, and to make sure that no one went without proper housing, fuel and care. "Wonderful charitable people the Darwins were," said the village carpenter. "Used to give away penny tickets on bread for the baker. I've given away thousands and thousands. And very good to the poor for blankets and coal and money till they got run on" (Browne 2002, 452). Spurred by a similar philosophy, Thomas Henry Huxley, Darwin's "bulldog," he who invented the word agnostic," ran for and was elected to the first London School Board in 1871. "He opted for selective Bible-reading, 'without any comment,' to instill moral principles." A progressive Victorian but a Victorian nevertheless, Huxley insisted that the reading "be selective: the Old Testament was as much vice as virtue. Who would want the lasciviousness of Lot's daughters or Joseph's seduction taught?" (Desmond 1997, 403). In a late essay, Huxley went so far as to argue that morality is opposed to evolution and that we must strive against our innate animal drives (Huxley 1893).

This was hardly going to be Darwin's position. He had not labored his way through the *Origin* and half of the *Descent* to have to throw up his hands and say that his mechanism was opposed to the most important aspect of humankind. Against Huxley, the first thing that Darwin had to argue was that natural selection could lead to some kind of harmonious social situation. He had to argue that it is false that, from a biological perspective, the struggle just leads to outright hostility and competition and warfare, and that anything social must be imposed from without, almost by force as it were. Darwin had faced this problem in the *Origin* when dealing with the social insects. His solution there to the problem was to suggest that it comes about because of relatedness. Organisms show help to others if they are related. Although Darwin did not have the language of genetics, he would have agreed with today's thinkers who argue that, inasmuch as relatives reproduce, one is oneself reproducing by proxy, because you share units of heredity (genes) with relatives (Hamilton 1964a, b). Kin selection!

In the *Descent*, Darwin extended this discussion somewhat. He suggested that sociality could come through interaction of non-relatives, through what today is known as "reciprocal altruism" – you scratch my back and I will scratch yours (Trivers 1971). "In the first place, as the reasoning powers and foresight of the members became improved, each man would soon learn that if he aided his fellow-men, he would commonly receive aid in return. From this low motive he might acquire the habit of aiding his fellows; and the habit of performing benevolent actions certainly strengthens the feeling of sympathy which gives the first impulse to benevolent actions. Habits, moreover, followed during many generations probably tend to be inherited" (Darwin 1871, 1, 163–4). Then

Darwin added: "But there is another and much more powerful stimulus to the development of the social virtues, namely, the praise and the blame of our fellow-men. The love of approbation and the dread of infamy, as well as the bestowal of praise of blame, are primarily due, as we have seen in the third chapter, to the instinct of sympathy; and this instinct no doubt was originally acquired, like all the other social instincts, through natural selection" (1, 164). He elaborated: "To do good unto others – to do unto others as ye would they should do unto you, – is the foundation-stone of morality. It is, therefore, hardly possible to exaggerate the importance during rude times of the love of praise and the dread of blame" (1, 165).

Darwin elaborated. "It must not be forgotten that although a high standard of morality gives but a slight or no advantage to each individual man and his children over the other men of the same tribe, yet that an advancement in the standard of morality and an increase in the number of well-endowed men will certainly give an immense advantage to one tribe over another" (1, 166). There is no ambiguity about what this means: "There can be no doubt that a tribe including many members who, from possessing in a high degree the spirit of patriotism, fidelity, obedience, courage, and sympathy, were always ready to give aid to each other and to sacrifice themselves for the common good, would be victorious over most other tribes; and this would be natural selection." Hence, the consequence. "At all times throughout the world tribes have supplanted other tribes; and as morality is one element in their success, the standard of morality and the number of well-endowed men will thus everywhere tend to rise and increase." Let us emphasize that Darwin was not now breaking from the thinking of the *Origin*. Following the comparative jurist Henry Maine (1861), he regarded tribes as inter-related families (or thinking they are), and he took the family to be one individual, a kind of super-organism.[4] With respect to morality, humans are like the ants. We are parts of a whole rather than individuals doing their own thing (Richards and Ruse 2016). Note however that although we may have a super-organism, the parts are furthering their own ends and only incidentally that of the whole. I am better off being part of a tribe.

Moral philosophers make a distinction between substantive or normative ethics, what should I do, and metaethics, why should I do what I should do? Take Christianity. It has all sorts of normative dictates, not always consistent with each other. But central is the Love Commandment – love your neighbor as yourself. Why should you love your neighbor as yourself? Most Christians subscribe to some version of the Divine Command Theory. Because God wants

---

[4] Without comment, showing his agreement, Darwin inserted as a footnote: "After a time the members or tribes which are absorbed into another tribe assume, as Mr. Maine remarks (Ancient Law, 1861, 131), that they are the co-descendants of the same ancestors."

you to! "Who hath prevented me, that I should repay him? whatsoever is under the whole heaven is mine" (Job 41:11). For Darwin, there could be no such appeal. Although he writes the *Descent* as a scientist, not as a philosopher – strictly speaking he is not bound to answer these questions – it is not difficult to see where he stands. With respect to substantive ethics, we ought to do what our biology dictates: remember, "patriotism, fidelity, obedience, courage, and sympathy," combined with a readiness "to give aid to each other and to sacrifice themselves for the common good." Not to think and behave this way would go against our deepest nature. Not that we should be patsies. We know that Darwin was very much a child of his time, a time that saw Britain rising to the top of the heap thanks to the vigor of its industrialists, scientists, thinkers, politicians and more. The meek do not inherit the Earth. The men and women of guts and determination are not just the winners but in some real sense the people of moral worth. Think Thomas Henry Huxley (Desmond 1998). Rising from modest beginnings, he became a professor of anatomy, dean of the new science university in South Kensington, as noted member of the first London School Board, leader of government commissions, Privy Counselor, non-stop lecturer, and author of some of the greatest essays of all time. At the same time, he battled crushing depressions, refusing to let them triumph. Darwinian substantive ethics owes much to Christian ethics, but it is colored with the norms of Victorian society.

Darwinian metaethics is a bit trickier, but there are very suggestive clues. Darwin was a moral non-realist. He believed in substantive ethics, but he didn't think it had any external justification. Darwin owned and, between 1838 and 1840, read carefully Sir James Mackintosh's *Dissertation on the Progress of Ethical Philosophy Chiefly During the Seventeenth and Eighteenth Centuries*, which discusses the thinking of David Hume, Adam Smith and others (Darwin 1987). Little surprise then that Darwin was in the same school as the mid-twentieth century emotivists and prescriptivists, going back to David Hume (Ruse 1986a). Darwin calmly pointed out that, had our evolution been otherwise, our moral understanding would be very different. Were it the case that "men were reared under precisely the same conditions as hive-bees, there can hardly be a doubt that our unmarried females would, like the worker-bees, think it a sacred duty to kill their brothers, and mothers would strive to kill their fertile daughters; and no one would think of interfering." This would rise above blind behavior: "the bee, or any other social animal, would in our supposed case gain, as it appears to me, some feeling of right and wrong, or a conscience" (Darwin 1871, 1, 74–75). Let us stress precisely what this means. It does not mean that substantive morality is made up, or that it is all relative, or that if it feels okay then it is okay. We are evolved social creatures. We ourselves did not make up our morality. It was fashioned long before we were born. Within our society there is no relativism at this level. The person who goes against the norm is going to get punished or kicked out. We are humans not ants, and, so as far as we are concerned, that is that. Brothers can rest easy!

4 Herbert Spencer

Charles Darwin was not the first or only evolutionist when he was discovering his theory. Mentioned already is his grandfather, Erasmus Darwin, who pushed evolutionary ideas at the end of the eighteenth century. In the 1840s, there was the *Vestiges of the Natural History of Creation*, anonymously published but as we now know authored by the Scottish publisher Robert Chambers. Drawing down scorn from the professional scientific community, Chambers offered a veritable gallimaufry of ideas about organic change. This opprobrium was probably a major factor in Darwin's delaying publication, although, interestingly, the major poet of the day, Alfred Tennyson, picked up on Chambers' ideas in his poem *In Memoriam* (1850), a tribute to a dead friend of his youth. Depressed by the seemingly meaninglessness of it all – it was he who popularized the famous phrase about "nature red in tooth and claw" – Tennyson then found optimistic relief in Chambers' thinking, suggesting that perhaps this dead friend was a special superior being who came before his time. We have the prospect of (using a term from *Vestiges*) a "crowning race."

> Whereof the man, that with me trod
> This planet, was a noble type
> Appearing ere the times were ripe,
> That friend of mine who lives in God.

All paled however compared to the indefatigable Herbert Spencer, who burst on the scene around 1850 and who was still promoting his "Synthetic Philosophy" at and beyond the century's end. He made no bones about his evolutionism. "Those who cavalierly reject the Theory of Evolution as not being adequately supported by facts, seem to forget that their own theory is supported by no facts at all. Like the majority of men who are born to a given belief, they demand the most rigorous proof of any adverse belief, but assume that their own needs none" (Spencer 1852b). What about mechanisms? At one point, years after Darwin discovered it, but nearly a decade before the *Origin*, Spencer floated a form of natural selection. Even – unlike Wallace for example (who never liked the breeding analogy) – using the word "select." Life is an ongoing battle. "All mankind in turn subject themselves more or less to the discipline described; they either may or may not advance under it; but, in the

nature of things, only those who do advance under it eventually survive."
Continuing:

> This truth we have recently seen exemplified in Ireland. And here, indeed,
> without further illustration, it will be seen that premature death, under all its
> forms, and from all its causes, cannot fail to work in the same direction. For
> as those prematurely carried off must, in the average of cases, be those in
> whom the power of self-preservation is the least, it unavoidably follows, that
> those left behind to continue the race are those in whom the power of self-
> preservation is the greatest—are the select of their generation. (Spencer
> 1852a, 500)

Spencer, however, was never a Darwinian, proto or otherwise. Like Darwin
(and Wallace) he started with the Malthusian potential population increase and
consequent struggle. But he saw this primarily as a spur to greater effort and
improvement, which then would be transmitted to later generations through
Lamarckian processes, the inheritance of acquired characteristics. And thus
would come ever-greater change. To quote the sentences immediately after the
passage just quoted: "So that, whether the dangers to existence be of the kind
produced by excess of fertility, or of any other kind, it is clear, that by the
ceaseless exercise of the faculties needed to contend with them, and by the death
of all men who fail to contend with them successfully, there is ensured
a constant progress towards a higher degree of skill, intelligence, and self-
regulation—a better co-ordination of actions—a more complete life." Already
selection per se is being ignored and "ceaseless exercise" is taking first place.

With all of this, fertility rates start to moderate and population pressures
decrease. With the growth in brain size the fertility falls away and the
Malthusian consequences are reduced. "Undue production of sperm-cells
involves cerebral inactivity. The first result of a morbid excess in this direction
is headache, which may be taken to indicate that the brain is out of repair; this is
followed by stupidity; should the disorder continue, imbecility supervenes,
ending occasionally in insanity" (Spencer 1852a, 493) One should take note
that Spencer himself was sufficiently advanced that, headaches or not, he had no
children at all. Before we get to this high point, however, there has been (and
continues to be), as this process takes place, a bloody struggle for existence and,
in Spencer's treatment of this, we see the seeds of traditional social Darwinism.
He writes of "spurious philanthropists" who try to alleviate the sufferings of the
poor through state aid, like the Poor Laws.

> Blind to the fact that under the natural order of things, society is constantly
> excreting its unhealthy, imbecile, slow, vacillating, faithless members, these
> unthinking, though well-meaning, men advocate an interference which not

> only stops the purifying process but even increases the vitiation—absolutely encourages the multiplication of the reckless and incompetent by offering them an unfailing provision, and discourages the multiplication of the competent and provident by heightening the prospective difficulty of maintaining a family. (Spencer 1851, 323–324)

You may think that this is all truly dreadful. How can anyone almost relish the suffering and misery that the natural course of events is going to bring on our fellow humans? The answer lies in flipping from what we have seen, what we might call his normative ethics, to Spencer's justification, his metaethics. Progress! Drawing on German sources – Friedrich Schelling notably – Spencer saw progress (in the organic world) as marked by a kind of increasing complexification. "It is settled beyond dispute that organic progress consists in a change from the homogeneous to the heterogeneous." Spencer then broadened from the organic to the social.

> Now, we propose in the first place to show, that this law of organic progress is the law of all progress. Whether it be in the development of the Earth, in the development of Life upon its surface, in the development of Society, of Government, of Manufactures, of Commerce, of Language, Literature, Science, Art, this same evolution of the simple into the complex, through successive differentiations, holds throughout. From the earliest traceable cosmical changes down to the latest results of civilization, we shall find that the transformation of the homogeneous into the heterogeneous, is that in which Progress essentially consists . . ..
> It is clearly enough displayed in the progress of the latest and most heterogeneous creature – Man. It is alike true that, during the period in which the Earth has been peopled, the human organism has grown more heterogeneous among the civilized divisions of the species; and that the species, as a whole, has been growing more heterogeneous in virtue of the multiplication of races and the differentiation of these races from each other. (Spencer 1857, 244)

It is the prospect of progress that justifies the struggle for existence in the social world, permitting a laissez-faire society of the harshest kind.

Ethical justification drops right out of this mix. Spencer argued that morality emerges through the evolutionary process and our duties are to ensure that this happens by removing barriers and facilitating the process. "Ethics has for its subject-matter, that form which universal conduct assumes during the last stages of its evolution" (Spencer 1879, 21). Continuing: "And there has followed the corollary that conduct gains ethical sanction in proportion as the activities, becoming less and less militant and more and more industrial, are such as do not necessitate mutual injury or hindrance, but consist with, and are furthered by, co-operation and mutual aid." (See Ruse 2021 for more detail, including discussion of the essential differences between Darwin and Spencer.)

5 Social Darwinism Triumphant

We are now apparently off and running for a half century or more of traditional social Darwinism. In America, particularly. Given the gladiatorial society in which they lived, not a few in the New World responded enthusiastically to the Spencerian philosophy. Prominent were those titans of industry and trade, Andrew Carnegie, the great steel magnate, and John D. Rockefeller, of Standard Oil fame, who were enthusiasts – "The law of competition may be sometimes hard for the individual, [but] it is best for the race, because it insures the survival of the fittest in every department" (Carnegie 1889, 655). Showing how invariant is human nature, they found supporting voices in the professoriate. "A drunkard in the gutter is just where he ought to be ... The law of survival of the fittest was not made by man, and it cannot be abrogated by man. We can only, by interfering with it, produce the survival of the unfittest" (Sumner 1914).

Often fiction is our best guide.

> His teeth closed on Spitz's left fore leg. There was a crunch of breaking bone, and the white dog faced him on three legs. Thrice he tried to knock him over, then repeated the trick and broke the right fore leg. Despite the pain and helplessness, Spitz struggled madly to keep up. He saw the silent circle, with gleaming eyes, lolling tongues, and silvery breaths drifting upward, closing in upon him as he had seen similar circles close in upon beaten antagonists in the past. Only this time he was the one who was beaten.
>
> There was no hope for him. Buck was inexorable. Mercy was a thing reserved for gentler climes. (London 1903, 24)

The result is nigh inevitable.

> Spitz quivered and bristled as he staggered back and forth, snarling with horrible menace, as though to frighten off impending death. Then Buck sprang in and out; but while he was in, shoulder had at last squarely met shoulder. The dark circle became a dot on the moon-flooded snow as Spitz disappeared from view. Buck stood and looked on, the successful champion, the dominant primordial beast who had made his kill and found it good. (London 1903, 24).

This is from *The Call of the Wild,* by Spencer-enthusiast Jack London. Before you start sneering at the crudity of our great-grandparents, we would point out that today there are over thirty – thirty! – editions of this book still in print.

There were those happy to see all of this in human terms. Such, for instant, were the sentiments of Theodore Roosevelt, the future president of the United States of America.

> The twentieth century looms before us big with the fate of many nations. If we stand idly by, if we seek merely swollen, slothful ease and ignoble peace, if we shrink from the hard contests where men must win at hazard of their lives and at the risk of all they hold dear, then the bolder and stronger peoples will pass us by, and will win for themselves the domination of the world. Let us therefore boldly face the life of strife, resolute to do our duty well and manfully; resolute to uphold righteousness by deed and by word; resolute to be both honest and brave, to serve high ideals, yet to use practical methods. Above all, let us shrink from no strife, moral or physical, within or without the nation, provided we are certain that the strife is justified, for it is only through strife, through hard and dangerous endeavor, that we shall ultimately win the goal of true national greatness. (Roosevelt 1899)

Teddy Roosevelt was a mere amateur compared to the Germans. Their social Darwinism did not, single-handedly, bring about the First World War, but it certainly helped (Evans 1997). General Friedrich von Bernhardi, pushed out of the German army because he was signaling a little too bluntly the General Staff's intentions, left no place for the imagination in his best-selling *Germany and the Next War* (1912). "War is a biological necessity," and hence: "Those forms survive which are able to procure themselves the most favourable conditions of life, and to assert themselves in the universal economy of nature. The weaker succumb." Progress depends on war: "Without war, inferior or decaying races would easily choke the growth of healthy budding elements, and a universal decadence would follow." And, anticipating horrible philosophies of the twentieth century: "Might gives the right to occupy or to conquer. Might is at once the supreme right, and the dispute as to what is right is decided by the arbitrament of war. War gives a biologically just decision, since its decision rests on the very nature of things" (Bernhardi 1912, 10, quoted by Crook 1994, 83).

Von Bernhardi knew the real opponent of Germany – Britain! Magnanimously in a book published at the beginning of the war – *Our Future: A Word of Warning to the German Nation* – which the translator somewhat inventively rendered as – *Britain as Germany's Vassal* – he set out the conditions needed to avoid war between the two countries. For a start: "England would have to give Germany an absolutely free hand in all questions touching European politics, and agree beforehand to any increase of Germany's power on the Continent of Europe which may ensue from the formation of a Central European Union of Powers, or from a German war with France" (von

Bernhardi 1914, 152). From Elizabethan times or earlier, British diplomacy had centered on not letting any single European state dominate all the others. Von Bernhardi obviously knew that his suggestions would not be taken seriously. Other demands were equally fanciful. A dominant, sea-faring empire like Britain was never going to let Germany to do what it liked in Africa and Asia. And only someone living in cloud-cuckoo land would think Britain would be indifferent to the rise and activity of the German navy. Indeed, from the end of the nineteenth century there had been an ever-increasing naval arms race between the two countries. Von Bernhardi was setting up a straw man. This done, von Bernhardi took careful aim and gave his solution. Germany must arm, rearm, and arm some more. War is needed. War is inevitable.

Take note of the appeal to the organic nature of the state and how it leads to struggle with others. "Every nation possesses an individuality of its own, and all progress among nations is based on their competition among themselves. As the competition among nations leads occasionally and unavoidably to differences among them, all real progress is founded upon the struggle for existence and the struggle for power prevailing among them." This is a good thing. "That struggle eliminates the weak and used-up nations, and allows strong nations possessed of a sturdy civilisation to maintain themselves and to obtain a position of predominant power until they too have fulfilled their civilising task and have to go down before young and rising nations" (26).

Came the war and von Bernhardi's dog was licked. The old general was unregenerate. Germany's defeat came entirely through mismanagement, and – anticipating a lament that was going to be made repeatedly by the National Socialists – the Versailles Treaty limiting Germany's right to a standing army is an abomination. If there is trouble ahead, it will be the fault of the conquerors not the vanquished. Bernhardi's philosophy of struggle and conflict was unchanged. "Always, as long as humans are humans, force in its most encompassing sense will indicate the political and cultural meaning of states. It is at the root of all mental and moral progress" (von Bernhardi 1920, 237). Note the yearning for progress. War is not a good in its own right. It is rather that it leads to the desired kind of change – upwards.

6 Rejection

We have now seen the positive case for social Darwinism. Look now at the other side. Why now does it have such an awful reputation? Some of the reason is more internal, some more external. Starting with the most obvious of the internal, there were some dreadful practices associated with the philosophy. Andrew Carnegie, to give one prominent instance, was associated with some of the worst management-worker excesses of the day. Especially notable was the Homestead Strike in Pittsburgh of 1892, pitting the Amalgamated Association of Iron and Steel Workers against the Carnegie Steel Company. Admittedly the day-to-day running of the company's fight against the workers lay with Carnegie's partner Henry Clay Frick, but either way the conflict was dreadful, with three hundred imported (from NYC) Pinkerton agents brought in to protect non-union strike breakers. Ten men were killed in subsequent clashes. In the end, the union was broken and work continued with non-union immigrant workers. (Remember, this was the time of vast immigrant numbers from Italy and Eastern Europe and the like.) For many, Carnegie was tainted for life. And the same goes for social Darwinism, however called.

Even more suspect and reviled than American capitalism was German militarism. There is much debate about the causes of the First World War, although general opinion is that German militarism (as flagged by von Bernhardi) was a major, if not the major, contributing factor (Ruse 2018). Whatever the right answer, as soon as the conflict began, scapegoats had to be found, and the German High Command – of which von Bernhardi had been a member – conveniently offered itself. It did not help its case with appalling atrocities as it marched the army through Belgium in the fall of 1914, on its way down to France – and, as it turned out, the four-year stalemate of the trenches. Doing really stupid things like shooting the English nurse, Edith Cavell, for aiding escapees – a propaganda coup for the British that resonates to this day with her statue in Trafalgar Square – and the pie was well and truly cooked. This impression of the Germans as out-of-control Darwinians was widely circulated thanks to the efforts of the American evolutionary biologist Vernon Kellogg. In the early years of the War, Kellogg (doing relief work in Europe) messed with the German High Command in Belgium, even meeting the Kaiser on one occasion. (He was able to do this because America did not join the War until 1917.) What he heard so shocked him that he relinquished his pacifism and wrote a little book, *Headquarters Nights*, that told the world of the vile social doctrines of Germany's leaders. Little wonder that social Darwinism got a bad name.

> For their point of view does not permit of a live-and-let-live kind of carrying on. It is a point of view that justifies itself by a whole-hearted acceptance of the worst of Neo-Darwinism, the Allmacht of natural selection applied rigorously to human life and society and Kultur.
>
> The creed of the Allmacht of a natural selection based on violent and fatal competitive struggle is the gospel of the German intellectuals; all else is illusion and anathema.

Struggle – bitter, ruthless struggle – is the rule among the different human groups. This struggle not only must go on, for that is the natural law, but it should go on, so that this natural law may work out in its cruel, inevitable way the salvation of the human species. By its salvation is meant its desirable natural evolution. That human group which is in the most advanced evolutionary stage as regards internal organization and form of social relationship is best, and should, for the sake of the species, be preserved at the expense of the less advanced, the less effective.

This is the disheartening kind of argument that I faced at Headquarters. (Kellogg 1917, 28)

No wonder that Darwinism, as applied to our species, had a bad name. Not entirely irrelevantly, one should note that, although Kellogg was an enthusiastic evolutionist, he had never much cared for Darwinism. Indeed, in *Darwinism Today* (1905), a widely read account of evolution and its causes, he had written: "Darwinism, as the all-sufficient or even most important causo-mechanical factor in species-forming and hence as the sufficient explanation of descent, is discredited and cast down." In throwing Darwinism overboard – or rather, in ascribing it to the German military – Kellogg was simply expanding a view he had always held. (Kellogg was not alone in rejecting Darwin's theory. More later on this point.)

A second reason for the decline and fall of social Darwinism revolved around something more external, in the sense that this was something more impinging on social Darwinism than something emanating from it. The question of progress. We have seen how progress was the metaethical justification behind almost all arguments for an evolutionary perspective. If Darwin in the *Descent* is an exception, we can respond that he was not himself giving a philosophical analysis of morality, but a scientific account of how it came about. Certainly, for conventional social Darwinism, progress was at the center of the case. What if progress proved chimerical? What if there was no genuine progress? By the end of the nineteenth century, many were starting to suspect precisely that. The terrible slums in the major cities of the land; the horrendously costly militarization – the naval arms race between Britain and Germany being a prime example; the costs of Empire – the Boer War on the horizon; the degeneracy of art – think Oscar Wilde; and so much more. Little wonder that Thomas Henry Huxley had warned that we must fight the tiger and lion within. By the end of his life, he didn't see a lot of progress in evolution.

Neither did two of his most famous students. E. Ray Lankester was a prominent if controversial biologist at the end of the nineteenth century. Among other positions he held was that of Director of the British Museum. Later in life, he became a widely read columnist for the *Daily Telegraph* newspaper. He worried desperately about the possibilities of degeneration. One should say that Lankester had personal, private reasons for such worries (Ruse 1996). He was unable to get an erection in the company of women of his own middle class and could do so only with prostitutes. He thought this was the result of an all-male upbringing, first at school and then at university. Be this as it may, sexual relief was to be found only on furtive visits to Paris and its brothels. And intellectual relief was to be found in his writings. Take the barnacle. It degenerates in its life from a happy, little, free-moving, marine organism to a pathetic remnant stuck to a ship and able only to grab and eat. "After swimming about for a time the Barnacle's Nauplius fixes its head against a piece of wood, and takes to a perfectly fixed, immobile state of life and that is it. Its organs of touch and of sight atrophy, its legs lose their locomotor function, and are simply used for bringing floating particles to the orifice of the stomach; so that an eminent naturalist has compared one of these animals to a man standing on his head and kicking his food into his mouth" (Lankester 1880, 37).

Degeneration! Can we avoid entertaining the possibility that we of the superior human races are on the same downward path? "With regard to ourselves, the white races of Europe, the possibility of degeneration seems to be worth some consideration. In accordance with a tacit assumption of universal progress – an unreasoning optimism – we are accustomed to regard ourselves as necessarily progressing, as necessarily having arrived at a higher and more elaborated condition than that which our ancestors reached, and as destined to progress still further." Fair enough. Yet, "it is well to remember that we are subject to, the general laws of evolution, and are as likely to degenerate as to progress." The English public-school system may have made Lankester a sexual cripple; it also made him knowledgeable about the classics. Dare we today say we are better than the Greeks of old? "Does the reason of the average man of civilised Europe stand out clearly as an evidence of progress when compared with that of the men of bygone ages?" Indeed: "Possibly we are all drifting, tending to the condition of intellectual Barnacles or Ascidians" (60).

Gloomy? But perhaps not as gloomy as the fiction of another of Huxley's students, the novelist H. G. Wells. The *Time Machine* is classic. The traveler goes off into the future where he finds a land with two human-like species – the Eloi and the Morlocks. Both are degenerate. The Eloi are beautiful and worthless. "A queer thing I soon discovered about my little hosts, and that was their lack of interest. They would come to me with eager cries of astonishment, like children, but, like children they would soon stop examining me, and wander away after some other toy." It's all a Darwinian nightmare. Instead of moving up the scale from female to male, as suggested by the *Descent of Man*, the sexes have given up the struggle. "Seeing the ease and security in which these people were living, I felt that this close resemblance of the sexes was after all what one would expect; for the strength of a man and the softness of a woman, the institution of the family, and the differentiation of occupations are mere militant necessities of an age of physical force" (Wells 1895, 29–30). Even the girlfriend is a mixed blessing. "She was exactly like a child. She wanted to be with me always. She tried to follow me everywhere, and on my next journey out and about it went to my heart to tire her down, and leave her at last, exhausted and calling after me rather plaintively."

Then there is the other group, the Morlocks. They are hard workers. Not beautiful though. Living underground they resemble stunted miners, which is what in fact they have become. Except worse by far. What did they eat? "I tried to look at the thing in a scientific spirit. After all, they were less human and more remote than our cannibal ancestors of three or four thousand years ago. And the intelligence that would have made this state of things a torment had gone. Why should I trouble myself? These Eloi were mere fatted cattle, which the ant-like Morlocks preserved and preyed upon—probably saw to the breeding of" (79). Not much progress here. Nor is there more when the traveler goes further in time. He sits on the beach.

> I saw that, quite near, what I had taken to be a reddish mass of rock was moving slowly towards me. Then I saw the thing was really a monstrous crab-like creature. Can you imagine a crab as large as yonder table, with its many legs moving slowly and uncertainly, its big claws swaying, its long antennæ, like carters' whips, waving and feeling, and its stalked eyes gleaming at you on either side of its metallic front? Its back was corrugated and ornamented with ungainly bosses, and a greenish incrustation blotched it here and there. I could see the many palps of its complicated mouth flickering and feeling as it moved. (83)

Enough! Fiction certainly! Truth about ourselves? Very possibly. Not much hope for a moral system with this sort of thing as its foundation.

Then there were the philosophers. They did not like social Darwinism. William James wrote of Roosevelt that he was "still mentally in the *Sturm und Drang* period of early adolescence" (Hofstadter 1944, 195). James' fellow Pragmatist, John Dewey, was no more favorable. About an evolution-inspired, laissez-faire view of society, he wrote: "Such a theory, in and of itself, is a literary diversion for those who, not being competent in the fields of outer achievement, amuse themselves by idealizing it in writing. Like most literary versions of science, it rests upon a pseudo-science, a parody of the real facts" (Hofstadter 1944, 371). Dewey stressed that this was a reading not sanctioned by Darwin's writings but came from others. England also had its critics. Henry Sidgwick was the leading British moral philosopher of the late nineteenth century. He made no bones about his position. "It is more necessary to argue that the theory of Evolution, thus widely understood, has little or no bearing upon ethics." Continuing that he had nothing against evolution as such, "but when it is all admitted, I cannot see that any argument is gained for or against any particular ethical doctrine." In other words, it is wrong to go from the origin of moral thinking to justification for moral thinking. It is a version of the genetic fallacy, thinking the route to discovery of an idea has relevance for the justification of that idea. Sidgwick continues to shove in the knife. He spots that the metaethical justification of the substantival claims of evolutionary ethics – although he mentions Darwin, Spencer is his main victim – is progress. But biological sense does not imply progress in a moral sense.

> Probably all who speak of Evolution mean by it not merely a process from old to new, but also a progress from less to more of certain qualities or characteristics. But that these characteristics are intrinsically good or desirable is more often implied than explicitly stated: otherwise it would be more clearly seen that this ethical proposition cannot be proved by any of the physical reasonings commonly used to establish the doctrine of Evolution. (Sidgwick 1876, 56)

The biological simply does not imply the moral. "But the fact is that in the ordering of an individual man's life, Development or Perfection of Organisation scarcely comes into competition with Happiness as an end of action" (61).

Sidgwick was not alone in his scornful attitude to thinking in the Herbert Spencer mode. Arthur Balfour was a British politician, sometime Prime Minister, best known for the "Balfour Declaration" of 1917, which gave support for a Jewish homeland in then-Arab territories. He was also a sophisticated philosopher, who first formulated the evolutionary argument against naturalism, namely that evolution undermines the stability of our beliefs, so in a way naturalism is self-refuting. In recent years, without crediting his predecessor, the Calvinist philosopher Alvin Plantinga has made much of this argument. What evolution does not do is throw much light on philosophical issues about morality.

> For not only does there seem to be no ground, from the point of view of biology, for drawing a distinction in favour of any of the processes, physiological or psychological, by which the individual or the race is benefited ; not only are we bound to consider the coarsest appetites, the most calculating selfishness, and the most devoted heroism, as all sprung from analogous causes and all evolved for similar objects, but we can hardly doubt that the august sentiments which cling to the ideas of duty and sacrifice are nothing better than a device of Nature to trick us into the performance of altruistic actions. (Balfour 1895, 16)

And so to G. E. Moore and *Principia Ethica* (1903). Writing in the tradition of Sidgwick, who in turn was drawing on insights of David Hume, Moore derided the mistaken attempt to go from claims about matters of fact to claims about matters of obligation: "Ethics aims at discovering what are those other properties belonging to all things which are good. But far too many philosophers have thought that when they named those other properties they were actually defining good; that these properties, in fact, were simply not 'other,' but absolutely and entirely the same with goodness. This view I propose to call the 'naturalistic fallacy'" (Moore 1903, 10). Unsurprisingly, Herbert Spencer is identified as a grave offender.

> There can be no doubt that Mr Spencer has committed the naturalistic fallacy. All that the Evolution-Hypothesis tells us is that certain kinds of conduct are more evolved than others; and this is, in fact, all that Mr Spencer has attempted to prove in the two chapters concerned. Yet he tells us that one of the things it has proved is that conduct gains ethical sanction in proportion as it displays certain characteristics. (31)

Continuing:

> It may, of course, be true that what is more evolved is also higher and better. But Mr Spencer does not seem aware that to assert the one is in any case not the same thing as to assert the other. He argues at length that certain kinds of conduct are 'more evolved,' and then informs us that he has proved them to gain ethical sanction in proportion, without any warning that he has omitted the most essential step in such a proof. Surely this is sufficient evidence that he does not see how essential that step is. (31)

We need not make bricks from straw. The identification of evolutionary approaches to ethics with truly vile social prescriptions, the decline of enthusiasm for progress, the blatant failure to recognize fallacious thinking – after all this, it is little wonder that social Darwinism (however called) had a bad name and an ever-declining group of supporters. Story over!

7 Darwin and Spencer Redux

What does one say to this onslaught? In the light of Moore's critique, there is an obvious counter, employed most egregiously by the older author of this Element (Ruse 1986a). Charles Darwin, like Mother Teresa, is beyond criticism. It's all Herbert Spencer's fault! Anyone who can write of society "excreting" people has much to answer for, including the policies of the National Socialists. But is this true? Let us leave the saints to the Catholic Church. What about Darwin? It doesn't take much digging to discover that, in many respects, his social beliefs and prescriptions were not that much different from Spencer, except Darwin wrote from the perspective of the rich upper-middle classes, whereas (as we shall see) Spencer was making the case from a segment of society that in many justifiable respects felt excluded. Darwin's theory was not that of Spencer. He did not buy into all the guff about stress leading to higher forms; although Darwin was always empathetic to Lamarckism, natural selection was ever central. But in many respects, there was a shared political philosophy. "I could show fight on natural selection having done and doing more for the progress of civilisation than you seem inclined to admit. Remember what risks the nations of Europe ran, not so many centuries ago of being over-whelmed by the Turks, and how ridiculous such an idea now is. The more civilised so-called Caucasian races have beaten the Turkish hollow in the struggle for existence. Looking to the world at no very distant date, what an endless number of the lower races will have been eliminated by the higher civilised races throughout the world" (Letter 13230, Darwin Correspondence Project, to William Graham, July 3, 1881).

In his own society also, Darwin wanted no constraints on laissez-faire, especially if they were going to crimp the welfare of folks like the Darwins who were living off the labors of the lower classes. Although the Darwin family (and his mother and wife's family, the Wedgwoods) were violently against slavery, there was not much love of unions. Writing to a German correspondent in 1872, Darwin said: "I much wish that you would sometimes take occasion to discuss an allied point, if it holds good on the continent,— namely the rule insisted on by all our Trades-Unions, that all workmen,— the good and bad, the strong and weak,— sh[oul]d all work for the same number of hours and receive the same wages." Adding: "I fear that Cooperative Societies, which many look at as the main hope for the future, likewise exclude competition. This seems to me a great evil for the future progress of mankind" (Darwin 1985, 20, 324). Add to this a partisan enthusiasm for the benefits of capitalism, and the pie is complete. "In all civilised countries man accumulates property and bequeaths it to his children." Adding: "But this is far from an unmixed evil; for without the accumulation of capital the arts could not progress; and it is chiefly through their power that the civilised races have extended, and are now everywhere extending, their range, so as to take the place of the lower races" (Darwin 1871, 1, 169). An element of self-interest seems to have been at work here in the thinking of the family-riches-supported Charles Darwin. "The presence of a body of well-instructed men, who have not to labour for their daily bread, is important to a degree which cannot be over-estimated; as all high intellectual work is carried on by them, and on such work material progress of all kinds mainly depends, not to mention other and higher advantages" (169).

What about progress? Darwin did not believe in any necessary progress, certainly not necessary progress of a Germanic kind. He certainly believed in progress as is shown by his comments just above about the Turks and "civilized races." He came to think that what we today call biological "arms races" can do the trick.

> If we look at the differentiation and specialisation of the several organs of each being when adult (and this will include the advancement of the brain for intellectual purposes) as the best standard of highness of organisation, natural selection clearly leads towards highness; for all physiologists admit that the specialisation of organs, inasmuch as they perform in this state their functions better, is an advantage to each being; and hence the accumulation of variations tending towards specialisation is within the scope of natural selection. (Darwin 1861, 134)

Spencer may have been the driving force, but anyone turning to Darwin himself would not have come away entirely empty-handed.

What then about the effects, the reactions to and uses made of the evolutionary philosophy coming out of these two men? Here too, the story is not quite what it is often taken to be.[5] Start with Spencer himself. Already, we ought to be feeling a little suspicious, if only because the whole point of his system is that the struggle will fade away and be unnecessary. This doesn't sound like the route to war, First or Second. (Incidentally, it doesn't sound like Darwin's route to war, either. He thought that concern for others would spread out and human conflict would decline.) As we start to uncover the full story, the tale starts to sound very different, especially starting with the fact that the horrendous quote about society "constantly excreting its unhealthy, imbecile, slow, vacillating, faithless members" was probably written before Spencer became a full-blown evolutionist. Really significant is the fact that Spencer was an enthusiast for organicism, arguing that the state is an integrated organism, with parts serving the whole. This overlap with von Bernhardi – for all that the contexts were different and Spencer was as anti-war as von Bernhardi was pro-war – was not fortuitous. Spencer's thinking reflected his debt to German philosophy – which he got through reading the nigh-plagiarized discussions of Romantic philosophy by the poet Samuel Coleridge— where there is great emphasis on the state as a unit (Ruse 2013). On the one hand, "the state is absolutely rational inasmuch as it is the actuality of the substantial will which it possesses in the particular self-consciousness once that consciousness has been raised to consciousness of its universality. This substantial unity is an absolute unmoved end

---

[5] R. J. Richards, *Darwin and the Emergence of Evolutionary Theories of Mind and Behavior* (1987) is the starting point for modern reassessments of Spencer.

in itself, in which freedom comes into its supreme right. On the other hand, this final end has supreme right against the individual, whose supreme duty is to be a member of the state" (Hegel 1821, 258).

We will pick up shortly on the Germans and the overlap with English thinking. Now, recognize that Spencer allowed that there can be intra-societal struggle within society. This does not break society apart; this improves it. Caution, however, must be taken with the comparison of the state with the individual organism. With the former, the state, the parts are physically separate. This is unlike biological organisms. "The parts of an animal form a concrete whole, but the parts of society form a whole which is discrete. While the living units composing the one are bound together in close contact, the living unit composing the other are free, are not in contact, and are more or less widely dispersed." Not to worry. Language steps up to the plate: "though the members of a social organism, not forming a concrete whole, cannot maintain cooperation by means of physical influences directly propagated from part to part, yet they can and do maintain cooperation by another agency. Not in contact, they nevertheless affect one another through intervening spaces, both by emotional language and by the language, oral and written of the intellect" (Spencer 1860).

Schelling wrote of "dynamic evolution" (Richards 1992). For Spencer, it all came together in a theory of "dynamic equilibrium," or, to use his term, "moving equilibrium." Organisms exist in a state of equilibrium. Then something comes along and disturbs this. Organisms regroup and move back to equilibrium. But not at the same level as before. The new state is in some sense higher. It is more complex, which in Spencer's language spells out as a move from homogeneity to heterogeneity: "that state of organic moving equilibrium which we saw arises in the course of Evolution, and tends ever to become more complete" (Spencer 1864, 1, 93). We know the proximate causes of this happening. Malthusian population pressures. Exactly why it happens in a wholescale fashion is a little less easy to fathom, but essentially Spencer regarded it as an a priori fact of nature. Things tend naturally away from simplicity to complexity, from the homogenous to the heterogenous. In tune with this, Spencer was always against militancy. In his youth, Spencer had been hustled off to Quaker meetings by his father. No surprise then that he thought the British-German naval arms race a waste of time and money. Going to the other side of the page, Spencer was in favor of free trade. Seizing on this notion, Immanuel Kant had written of the possibility of "eternal peace" (Kant 1795). Without feeling the need to acknowledge predecessors – Spencer was never too good on mentioning sources – the Englishman thought such commercial intercourse would encourage relationships between nations. In a kind of Darwinian reciprocal altruism fashion, we get the emergence of morality. With this comes the imperative to break down inter-societal barriers and to facilitate the process. Remember: "Ethics has for its subject-matter, that form which universal conduct assumes during the last stages of its evolution" (Spencer 1879, 21). Continuing: "conduct gains ethical sanction in proportion as the activities," become "less and less militant and more and more industrial, . . . "

From here, Spencer was led naturally to an analysis of the "militant society" as opposed to the "industrial society." Spencer may have drawn on German sources; he felt no need to temper anti-German criticism. "Such traits of the militant type in Germany as were before manifest, have, since the late war [the Franco-Prussian War of 1870–71], become still more manifest." Reverting to his own thinking and terminology, we learn that militant societies are more homogeneous whereas industrial societies are more heterogeneous. Militant societies may have had their role to play in the early stages of evolution. Today, they are otiose. Continuing in a Spencerian mode, the need of a struggle for existence will fade away. "But now observe that the inter-social struggle for existence which has been indispensable in evolving societies, will not necessarily play in the future a part like that which it has played in the past. Recognizing our indebtedness to war for forming great communities and developing their structures, we may yet infer that the acquired powers, available for other activities, will lose their original activities." It is accepted that "without these perpetual bloody strifes, civilized societies could not have arisen, and that an adapted form of human nature, fierce as well as intelligent, was a needful concomitant" – war in the past had its role and function. Now, however, with the arrival of modern societies, "the brutality of nature in their units which was necessitated by the process, ceasing to be necessary with the cessation of the process, will disappear" (Spencer 1882, 242).

This is a long way from the usual picture of Herbert Spencer's thinking about society. Someone determined to fault him can find incriminating passages. Spencer continued to believe that state help more often exacerbates suffering rather than ameliorates it. "Having, by unwise institutions, brought into existence large numbers who are unadapted to the requirements of social life, and are consequently sources of misery to themselves and others, we cannot repress and gradually diminish this body of relatively worthless people without inflicting much pain. Evil has been done and the penalty must be paid. Cure can come only through affliction" (Spencer 1892, 2, 394). Tough luck on the down-and-outs. But this does not mean that no one should do anything or that the aim is to bring unhappy states of affairs to an end. It is more a question of tactics.

Parenthetically, those who are reminded, by this Spencerian thinking, of the twentieth-century prime minister Margaret Thatcher are right on the mark. Like Spencer, she came from a lower-middle class, non-conformist (not Anglican) background in the British Midlands (a very industrial part of the country). Spencer and Thatcher both saw state interference as usually benefiting the rich and comfortable not the unwashed masses. They would have had in mind the Corn Laws enacted after the Napoleonic wars, that imposed a tariff on imported wheat (in England "corn" is wheat) when the price dropped below a certain level. This benefited the landowners and imposed costs on the laborer's loaf of bread. Government is not our friend. Better that some suffer than that all – other than the highest few – pay the cost. Paradoxically, in this political philosophy, the industry-owning Darwin family would have allied themselves with the Spencerians. The Corn Laws hurt business, because higher wages had to be paid. Later in the century, as the working class started to turn towards socialism, the remaining Liberals like the Darwins eventually joined forces with the land-owning Conservatives.

8 Social Darwinism Deconstructed

Move on to how these ideas were taken up by others and to do so move across the Atlantic. No one wants to deny that there was a fair amount of traditional social Darwinism thinking. But the story here also is more complex. Take Andrew Carnegie. We have seen his dark side, one so vile that he will always have the taint of cruel factory owner. There was, however, another side to this Scottish immigrant, a man who had made his way thanks solely to his own abilities. Carnegie thought so much about societal issues that he wrote a short book – *The Gospel of Wealth* – on the topic. A different picture starts to emerge. Certainly, Carnegie was fully convinced that traditional social Darwinism could not be – should not be – constrained, as this was the force for progress. To quote in full an abbreviated passage from earlier.

> The price which society pays for the law of competition, like the price it pays for cheap comforts and luxuries, is also great; but the advantages of this law are also greater still, for it is to this law that we owe our wonderful material development, which brings improved conditions in its train. But, whether the law be benign or not, we must say of it, as we say of the change in the conditions of men to which we have referred: It is here; we cannot evade it; no substitutes for it have been found; and while the law may be sometimes hard for the individual, it is best for the race, because it insures the survival of the fittest in every department. (Carnegie 1889, 655)

This, however, is but the start. The big question for Carnegie is: What do you do with all this wealth once you have accumulated it? He saw three responses. First, you do the traditional thing and leave it to your family. This is "most injudicious"! "Beyond providing for the wife and daughters moderate sources of income, and very moderate allowances indeed, if any, for the sons, men may well hesitate, for it is no longer questionable that great sums bequeathed oftener work more for the injury than for the good of the recipients." Carnegie knew all about idle playboys. The second is to leave your money at death for the furtherance of good and works. Bad idea! "Knowledge of the results of legacies bequeathed is not calculated to inspire the brightest hopes of much posthumous good being accomplished. The cases are not few in which the real object sought by the testator is not attained, nor are they few in which his real wishes are thwarted. In many cases the bequests are so used as to become only monuments of his folly." So this leaves the third option: use your money yourself for the good of society. "Under its sway we shall have an ideal state, in which the surplus wealth of the few will become, in the best sense the property of the many, because administered for the common good, and this wealth, passing through the hands of the few, can be made a much more potent force for the elevation of our race than if it had been distributed in small sums to the people themselves."

Carnegie is justly famous for his saying that "no man should die rich." He is as famous for putting his beliefs into practice and sponsoring the founding of public libraries. The older of the two authors spent many happy hours in the Carnegie library, in the British Midlands town of Walsall. He then went to work in Guelph, Ontario, home of another Carnegie library. Note how social Darwinian this all is. It is rather that the emphasis is more on enabling the success of the more talented, than simply allowing the failure of the less talented.[6] Note also how this fits with Spencer. A struggle with the consequent suffering is inevitable and has overall good effects. It does not mean that we should sit back, complacently, and just watch it happening. Incidentally, also the philosophy of Jack London, author of *Call of the Wild*. We left Buck triumphant over Spitz. Does he at once take advantage of his new authority, inseminating all the females in the pack? No, indeed! He turns into a high-school principal.

> Pike, who pulled at Buck's heels, and who never put an ounce more of his weight against the breast-band than he was compelled to do, was swiftly and repeatedly shaken for loafing; and ere the first day was done he was pulling more than ever before in his life. The first night in camp, Joe, the sour one, was punished roundly—a thing that Spitz had never succeeded in doing. Buck simply smothered him by virtue of superior weight, and cut him up till he ceased snapping and began to whine for mercy. (London 1903, 26)

---

[6] Modest bows by the senior author. The junior author, suspiciously silent, wishes now that he had not spent his youth playing video games.

In the words of Uncle Ben: "With great power comes great responsibility." In Darwinian language, what we seem to have here is less a cherishing of brute force for its own sake, and more a respect for vigor and a willingness to get out and do a job that ends by being for the benefit of us all.

Teddy Roosevelt also, on closer examination, seems not quite the Anglo-Saxon bully one might infer on a quick reading. "Side by side with the selfish development in life," Roosevelt tells us, "there has been almost from the beginning a certain amount of unselfish development too; and in the evolution of humanity the unselfish side has, on the whole, tended steadily to increase at the expense of the selfish, notably in the progressive communities." Those looking for crude endorsements of the struggle for existence are going to be out of luck. Such thinking leads to the erroneous conclusion that "the European peoples standing highest in the in the scale would be the south Italians, the Polish Jews, the people who live in the congested districts of Ireland. As a matter of fact, however, these are precisely the peoples who made the least progress when compared with the dominant strains among, for instance, the English and the Germans" (Burton 1965, 108). It is character that counts rather than intellect or a belligerent disposition. Much to be cherished was "the woman who watches over the sick child and the soldier who dies at his post" (107). No one denies the virtues of other aspects of human nature. "We need intellect, and there is no reason why we should not have it together with character; but if we must choose between the two, we choose character without a moment's hesitation." There is little surprise that Roosevelt did not put everything down to selection brought on by struggle. In essence, he was a Lamarckian before all else. "Even though the best people of society do not increase as fast as the others, society progresses, the improvement being due mainly to the transmission of acquired characteristics, a process which in every civilized society operates ... [in opposition to] ... the baleful law of natural selection" (109).[7]

9 Alternative Philosophies

Overall, the story is mixed. There is some heavy-duty evidence for traditional social Darwinism – more so perhaps than many revisionists are prepared to admit. This said, application of evolution to social issues was hardly the bogeyman that popular history would have it. In addition, at the risk of gilding the lily, several late-nineteenth century thinkers drew quite opposite conclusions about the necessity and worth of traditional social Darwinism. We have already encountered Thomas Henry Huxley, who thought progress is to be

---

[7] Burton quotes from a number of Roosevelt's essays, mainly one on "Social Evolution" (*Works* XIV).

achieved by denying our animal nature! "Man, the animal, in fact, has worked his way to the headship of the sentient world, and has become the superb animal which he is, in virtue of his success in the struggle for existence" (Huxley 1893, 51). Adding: "For his successful progress, throughout the savage state, man has been largely indebted to those qualities which he shares with the ape and the tiger; his exceptional physical organization; his cunning, his sociability, his curiosity, and his imitativeness; his ruthless and ferocious destructiveness when his anger is roused by opposition." Nevertheless, "in proportion as men have passed from anarchy to social organization, and in proportion as civilization has grown in worth, these deeply ingrained serviceable qualities have become defects. After the manner of successful persons, civilized man would gladly kick down the ladder by which he has climbed. He would be only too pleased to see "the ape and tiger die"" (52).

Huxley was scientific establishment. Let us now turn to a couple of outliers, one British, one Russian. Alfred Russel Wallace (1823–1913) could never hold a permanent job. With reason, people were not about to vest authority in him. He lived by his pen and by marking exam scripts. Later in life, the scientific community saw that he got a government pension. Wallace was several years younger than Darwin; he and Darwin were at opposite ends of the spectrum of the middle classes. Darwin was at the top. (Although very rich, Darwin was not upper class. That was for aristocrats and landed gentry.) Wallace was at the bottom. He used to joke that his solicitor father had no worries because there was no lower that he could sink (Wallace 1905). Wallace was a bit of a Jonah – if it could go wrong, it would go wrong. His middle name was spelt incorrectly on his birth certificate. On returning from a several-year collecting trip from South America, the ship burnt beneath him and he lost everything. His fiancée threw him over for another. He invested his funds in some stupid enterprise of a relative and ended up broke. And, of course, he discovered natural selection and then discovered he had been pipped by Darwin!

Fifteen years earlier than the evolution essay, in the 1840s, railways were being built everywhere so there was lots of work. Consequently, Wallace started his career as a surveyor. (Spencer also started on the railways before turning to writing.) Thrust alongside regular folk and becoming very conscious of the poverty of the rural poor, the fourteen-year-old Wallace was taken to hear the Scottish mill owner and socialist Robert Owen. It was a road-to-Damascus experience. He was thenceforth drawn strongly to community thinking. One consequence of which is that he always looked upon selection as a group phenomenon—which could include unrelated members. This is hinted by the title of the essay he first sent to Darwin in 1858: "On the Tendency of Varieties to Depart Indefinitely from the Original Type" (Wallace 1858; see also Ruse

1980). For Wallace, therefore, war within a species was always something counter to nature. It did not lead to fruitful evolutionary change. There could be no progress.

Like Darwin – indeed, inspiring Darwin in the *Descent* to explore the possibilities of sexual selection – Wallace saw humankind as "escaping" natural selection. For Wallace, however, sexual selection only compounds the problem. Intraspecific conflict is bad biologically and bad morally. "By his superior sympathetic and moral feelings, he [humankind] becomes fitted for the social state; he ceases to plunder the weak and helpless of his tribe; he shares the game which he has caught with less active or less fortunate hunters, or exchanges it for weapons which even the sick or the deformed can fashion; he saves the sick and wounded from death; and thus the power which leads to the rigid destruction of all animals who cannot in every respect help themselves, is prevented from acting on him" (Wallace 1864, clxviii). How then do we humans find ourselves so often at war? It is obviously a cultural or societal issue. However, whereas for Darwin it was something from which we escape thanks to civilization, for Wallace the reverse is true. It is imposed upon us by civilization. "Every addition of territory, every fresh conquest even of barbarous nations or of savages, provides outlets and additional places of power and profit for the ever-increasing numbers of the ruling classes, while it also provides employment and advancement for an increased military class in first subduing and then coercing the subject populations, and in preparing for the inevitable frontier disputes and the resulting further extensions of territory." Showing that he was not entirely at odds with (the also lower-middle-class) Spencer, Wallace stressed that it is the haves who get all of the benefits, and the have-nots who get stuck with the bills: "they invariably suffer from increased taxation, either temporarily or permanently, due to increased armaments, which the protection of the enlarged territory requires" (Wallace 1899, 213).

Wallace was acutely aware that he was not writing in a societal vacuum. Britannia rules the waves and there is altogether too much complacent satisfaction with the state of affairs. "We boast of our Empire on which 'the sun never sets'; and lose no opportunity of expressing our determination and vaunting our ability to keep it." Wallace disagreed strongly. "Again and again we have waged unjust wars, as those against China, Burma, Egypt, and North-West India; while our last exploit— the most unjust and disgraceful of all— was the conquest of the two Boer Republics, after a petty quarrel deliberately founded on fraud and aggression" (213). Wallace was no lover of a globe painted one-third red. Always attracted to the unpopular and derided – to the horror and scorn of his fellow scientists, he spent much of his life promoting that spiritualism so upsetting to Darwin – he was indifferent to the opprobrium that would fall on his head. One might add that, although Wallace was raised an Anglican, as with Spencer there seem to have been strong Quaker influences in his childhood (Shermer 2002, 48). Members of the Religious Society of Friends are known for their opposition to war.

From a different tradition, Prince Petr Kropotkin really was upper class. A Russian, an aristocrat, he was the child of a father who owned three hundred serfs. In his own way, he was as independent as Wallace. He broke with his background—notoriously, today he is still the most famous anarchist ever—and ended up being arrested and sent to the Peter and Paul prison in St. Petersburg. Escaping, Kropotkin went into exile in England. Always interested in science, it was there that he formulated and published his theory of "mutual aid," something that strongly reflected his Russian heritage (Todes 1989). For the British, the Malthusian population pressure was the starting point. They had a point. The way that numbers were rising was mind-boggling. The population of England doubled between 1781 (about seven million) and 1831 (about fourteen million). London alone grew from a million and a quarter in 1801 to over two million in 1831. No one needed convincing of the struggle for existence.

In Russia, things were very different. In essentially rural societies with limited land resources, as pre-industrial Britain had been, people tended to marry later and put off large families. In essentially urban societies, which post-industrial Britain became, often it was children who could best work in factories — tending weaving machines and the like. Hence, there were good economic reasons for many children, quickly. Russia was late to industrialize, and in any case the vast lands meant it was not space that was at a premium. What really mattered was the awful climate. One had no need of Dr. Zhivago to point out those harsh Russian winters. Hence, the real struggle occurred between organisms and the environment. The only way to survive – a belief that was general among Russian biologists and not exclusive to Kropotkin – was to work together. Reciprocal altruism. Help others and in turn expect help from others. "In the animal world we have seen that the vast majority of species live in societies and that they find in association the best arms for the struggle for life: understood, of course, in its wide Darwinian sense – not as a struggle for the sheer means of existence, but as a struggle against all natural conditions unfavourable to the species." This is not just a negative doctrine. "The animal species, in which individual struggle has been reduced to its narrowest limits, and the practice of mutual aid has attained the greatest development, are invariably the most numerous, the most prosperous, and the most open to further progress" (Kropotkin 1902, 158). Although for somewhat different reasons, as with Wallace, war was a disease of civilization, rather than something that civilization made outmoded. "One single war— we all know— may be productive of more evil, immediate and subsequent, than hundreds of years of the unchecked action of the mutual-aid principle may be productive of good" (159). War is a cancer on humankind. Save we recognize this, and take remedial steps, we have no hope of a better future.

Neither Wallace nor Kropotkin had the massive public profile of Herbert Spencer – few did, except the Royal Family and a handful of leading politicians – but they were well-known and had a solid readership. More than this, they represented a growing number of late-nineteenth-century thinkers who reacted against the individualism at the heart of the thinking of Darwin – that Malthusian struggle of one against one – and opted for a more community-type philosophy of society. Socialism! In England, one thinks particularly of the Fabian Society, driven above all by the husband-and-wife team of Sydney and Beatrice Webb. Wallace, expectedly, identified with these socialists, writing in his *Autobiography* (1905) that, although for years he had wrestled with his early convictions thanks to the "individualistic teachings of Mill and Spencer," such hesitancy was over: "in 1889, my views were changed once for all, and I have ever since been absolutely convinced, not only that socialism is thoroughly practicable, but that it is the only form of society worthy of civilized beings, and that it alone can secure for mankind continuous mental and moral advancement, together with that true happiness which arises from the full exercise of all their faculties for the purpose of satisfying all their rational needs, desires, and aspirations" (2, 266). Confirming the links between the New World and the Old, Wallace was converted by a futuristic novel, *Looking Backwards*, by the New Englander Edward Bellamy, supposedly showing the glories of socialism in the world of 2000.

This novelist was not alone. In his powerful work, *The Jungle,* dwelling on the appalling conditions of animals and men in the Chicago stockyards, Upton Sinclair played the same melody.

> Life was a struggle for existence, and the strong overcame the weak, and in turn were overcome by the strongest. Those who lost in the struggle were generally exterminated; but now and then they had been known to save themselves by combination— which was a new and higher kind of strength. It was so that the gregarious animals had overcome the predaceous; it was so, in human history, that the people had mastered the kings. The workers were simply the citizens of industry, and the Socialist movement was the expression of their will to survive. (Sinclair 1906, 273)

The thinking of the earlier-in-the-century, French positivist August Comte was a major influence on the development of socialism. In a private notebook we find Beatrice Webb translating and copying passages from the French thinker. "Our harmony as moral beings is impossible on any other foundation but altruism" (Dixon 2008, 247). "Altruism!" The use of this word warns us that one should not assume automatically that the discussions of the Victorians were always that evolution-infused, even if at times they gave the impression that they were. Defined in the early 1880s, by the newly appearing *Oxford Dictionary of the English Language*, as "Devotion to the welfare of others, regard for others as a principle of action; opposed to egoism or selfishness," there was ongoing discussion about whether altruism is or should be the ruling factor in human behavior. Either way, this did not originate as an evolutionary concept. It comes from positivism and, independently of evolutionary thinking, was introduced into Britain mid-century by people like G. H. Lewes, shortly to become the common-law husband of Mary Ann Evans, better known by her penname of George Eliot.

Not all evolutionists were enthused. It was never a term used by Darwin, and in his massive correspondence there is but one quick reference in a letter to him towards the end of his life. Herbert Spencer, part of the Lewes-Evans set – initially Evans had her eyes set on him! – took up the concept in some detail. In his *Data of Ethics* (1879), there is a lengthy (and rather good) discussion, contrasting altruism with egoism, arguing that, like Darby and Joan, you can't have one without the other. The person who tries to be exclusively altruistic is going to fail because they won't be happy in themselves. Conversely, the person who thinks only of self is going to be equally miserable. In his *Utilitarianism*, John Stuart Mill, another empathetic to positivism tells us that. "When people who are tolerably fortunate in their outward lot do not find in life sufficient enjoyment to make it valuable to them, the cause generally is caring for nobody but themselves" (Mill 1863, 20). It is another matter, however, as to how much of Spencer's approach to altruism is essentially due to an evolutionary commitment. He himself cautioned that one should take care about these sorts of supposed links. At most, "it helps us in general ways though not in special ways."

> In the first place, for certain modes of conduct which at present are supposed to have no sanction if they have not a supernatural sanction, it yields us a natural sanction–shows us that such modes of conduct fall within the lines of an evolving humanity–are conducive to a higher life, and are for this reason obligatory. In the second place, where it leaves us to form empirical judgments, it brings into view those general truths by which our empirical judgments should be guided–indicates the limits within which they are to be found. (Spencer 1892, 2, 6)

Socialism? Yes. Altruism? Yes. Influenced by Comte? Yes. A product of evolutionary thinking? Not quite so obvious. What we can say is that, whether the altruists are inside or outside the evolutionary loop, they challenged the hegemony of traditional social Darwinism. As did many who came to these issues from a Christian commitment. The end of the century saw the rise of the so-called "Social Gospel" movement, led by American Protestant ministers determined to revitalize Christianity and make it relevant to the times – speaking to the indifference already noted in mid-century by Charles Dickens – putting into practice the exhortations of Jesus to love and serve others. They reached out to the poor and suffering, trying to offer material help, at the same time making clear their opposition to the individual-centered philosophy of the social Darwinians. As the leading light of the movement, Congregationalist minister Washington Gladden, wrote in his informatively named *Christianity and Socialism*: "From the fact of the divine Fatherhood is derived the fact of human brotherhood. What the right relation of brothers must be, when the Fatherhood is divine, it is not easy to tell, though it is not hard to understand. Honor and obedience to the Father will rule all our conduct. We must therefore think his thoughts about our brothers; we must share in his purposes concerning them. The law of sympathy, of consideration, of helpful love, will be the law of all human association" (Gladden 1905, 2).

"The law of sympathy"? Not much for a "nature red in tooth and claw" world picture. Alternative philosophies, indeed!

10 Friedrich Nietzsche

By this point, more cosmopolitan readers will be feeling decidedly uneasy. We are missing the elephant in the room. What about the biggest social Darwinian of them all? He who, more than anyone, gave the movement a bad name. The biggest forerunner to and influence on the National Socialists? What about Friedrich Nietzsche? Well, what about Friedrich Nietzsche? Certainly, Nietzsche thought hard about the issues that so excised the evolutionists, morality and how we are to have and maintain it in a godless world of natural science. For Nietzsche, as much as for the Darwinians, it was a world "after Darwin." "We have unlearned something. We have become more modest in every way. We no longer derive man from the 'spirit,' from the 'god-head'; we have dropped him back among the beasts" (Nietzsche 1920, §14). The kind of world described by Darwin was a world in which Christian morality no longer made sense. For how could the kinds of moral imperatives typical of Christianity possibly arise in such a world? Talking about the imperative to treat others equally, Nietzsche asked:

> But whence sounds this imperative? How can man himself possess it, since, according to Darwin, he is precisely a creature of nature and nothing else, and has evolved to the height of being man by quite other laws: precisely, in fact,

by always forgetting that other creatures similar to him possessed equivalent rights, precisely by feeling himself the stronger, and gradually eliminating the other, weaker examples of his species? (Nietzsche 1983, §7)

We live in a very different kind of world after Darwin. It is no longer a world guided by the loving hand of a good God. That much is clear. "God is dead! God remains dead! And we have killed him – you and I" (Nietzsche 2001, §125). It is also clear that this fact has sweeping implications for morality: "now that this faith has been undermined, how much must collapse because it was built on this faith, leaned on it, had grown into it – for example, our entire European morality" (Nietzsche 2001, §343).

Of course, Nietzsche was well aware of the attempts made, on the part of "the English," to resuscitate some form of Christian morality in this new, Godless, Darwinian era. But was sharply critical of them. As he said about George Eliot:

> They are rid of the Christian God and now believe all the more firmly that they must cling to Christian morality. That is an English consistency . . . In England one must rehabilitate oneself after every little emancipation from theology by showing in a veritably awe-inspiring manner what a moral fanatic one is. That is the penance they pay there. We others hold otherwise. When one gives up the Christian faith, one pulls the right to Christian morality out from under one's feet. (Nietzsche 1954, Expeditions §5)

The same "English consistency," he thought, held true of Darwin and Spencer and other evolutionists, for each tried to show that morality – in the traditional, Christian sense – was a product of evolution, which meant that the death of God did not mean the death of morality as we knew it. Nietzsche saw all such as making the dishonest attempt to ground a Christian form of morality, with its emphasis on selflessness, in an evolutionary worldview grounded in self-interest. Each had failed to own up to the ultimate consequence of the death of God, which was the death of Christian morality, and instead had sought relief from this consequence in the idea that evolution could mold us into the good moral beings that God wanted us to be.

Very early on, Nietzsche concluded that evolutionary theory could not account for a Christian form of morality. In 1873, when he was just twenty-nine, he published a stinging rebuke of the German theologian-turned-scientist David Friedrich Strauss for trying to ground morality in evolution. Strauss' early (1835) book *The Life of Jesus* – the one translated by Mary Ann Evans – played a key role in Nietzsche's own loss of faith, but his later book *The Old Faith and the New* (1872) argued that atheism did not imply the loss of morality, for morality as we knew it – in the form of a categorical imperative to respect other human beings – could be derived from evolutionary theory (Strauss 1872, Vol. 2, 44–64). Despite Nietzsche's early admiration for Strauss, he could barely contain his contempt for this later work. He posed his objection in the form of a taunt. If Strauss really wanted to try lift a moral code off a descriptive account of the world, he should at least have the courage to embrace the true nature of the evolved world:

> With a certain rude contentment he covers himself in the hairy cloak of our ape-genealogists and praises Darwin as one of the greatest benefactors of mankind – but it confuses us to see that his ethics are constructed entirely independently of the question: 'What is our conception of the world?' Here was an opportunity to exhibit native courage: for here he ought to have turned his back on his 'we' and boldly derived a moral code for life out of the bellum omnium contra omnes and the privileges of the strong . . . (Nietzsche 1983, 29–30)

The only form of morality justified by Strauss' evolutionary view of nature – which was really more Hobbesian than Darwinian – was one of "might is right."

Nietzsche's criticisms of such attempts to retain Christian morality after the death of God have struck many as tantamount to an endorsement of this kind of "might is right" mentality – that is, the kind of mentality associated with supposed social Darwinism. Thomas Common, one of Nietzsche's earliest admirers, saw Nietzsche as embracing the Darwinian vision of the world as a place of struggle in a way that (for all the sentiments of his caste) Darwin himself did not do, supposedly calling for the eradication of Victorian morality in favor of a new ethic based on the principle of the acquisition of power (Common 1901). If nature was a kind of battleground in which the strongest and best adapted won out, then there must be some inherent value in having the strength and severity necessary to win the battle for resources among one's competitors. This reading – that although Christian morality cannot be got out of evolutionary thinking, a new "might is right" morality can be got out of such thinking – fits well with the popular understanding of Nietzsche as someone who thought that the rules of morality were conventions designed to stifle the strong, which should be overthrown so that the strong could pursue their interests untrammeled by the interests of the weak.

But while there is a respect for strength in his works, this is a fundamental misreading of Nietzsche's position – as it certainly is a fundamental misreading of Darwin and Spencer (Clark 1994). (To be candid, Nietzsche is so unpleasant about Darwin, it is small surprise there have been misreadings (Pence 2011).) Nietzsche's taunt to David Friedrich Strauss over the latter's failure to embrace an ethic based on the war of all against all was never intended as an endorsement of this kind of ethic. As Nietzsche would say later in the same essay, "an honest natural scientist believes that the world conforms unconditionally to laws, without however asserting anything as to the ethical or intellectual value of these laws" (Nietzsche 1983, 31). The fact that nature was characterized by a struggle for existence did not mean that such a struggle should be adopted as a new kind of moral code. Even less did it mean that we had to give up on morality altogether: "It goes without saying that I do not deny, presupposing I am no fool, that many actions called immoral ought to be avoided and resisted, or that many called moral ought to be done and encouraged–but for different reasons than formerly" (Nietzsche 1997, §103).

Nietzsche was no amoralist. Even if he sometimes billed himself as an "immoralist," what he really wanted was not to give up all forms of morality, but to replace our current, Christian form of it with a new form that would be better suited to the times. This was the move that he thought Eliot, Darwin, and Spencer had failed to make. The new kind of moral system that Nietzsche wanted was one according to which an action had value not insofar as it was altruistic, but insofar as it contributed to the flourishing of the self. In a sense, then, Nietzsche wanted to replace Christian morality with a more egoistic form of morality. But the kind of egoism he commended was of a higher or "ascending" variety, in contrast to the lower, "descending" variety (Nietzsche 1954, Expeditions §33). The lower form of egoism (which Nietzsche would have found in the Adam Smith / Charles Darwin notion of "self-interest), was the kind that Hobbes thought he saw in the state of nature, the kind that would result in a violent struggle between self-interested individuals to satisfy their own basic needs and desires. The higher form was one according to which one's strongest desires would often need to be checked against the pull of an ethically higher calling, which was the calling to "become who you are."

Nietzsche's supreme valuation of this good – the good of individuality – paralleled the thought of the Englishman John Stuart Mill. Nietzsche knew of Mill, but only as a Utilitarian democrat who claimed that pleasure was the supreme good. Insofar as Nietzsche deeply despised any claim that the good could be found in an easy life of pleasure or contentment, he assumed that Mill was an intellectual opponent, and treated him as such. About on a par with accusing Spencer of a crude form of altruism, when, in the *Data of Ethics*, Spencer went to some pains to show the dynamic between altruism and egoism. Had Nietzsche but read *On Liberty* (first published in 1859), he would have discovered that Mill was an intellectual ally. For like Nietzsche, Mill held that conformity to the masses was the chief disgrace for the individual, and a serious threat to social progress. In contrast, the formation of individual character was a supreme good, and a genuine spur to progress (Mill 1993).

Indeed, both Mill and Nietzsche held that the flourishing of the self – conceived as self-creation, or the creation of one's individual character – was not only compatible with, but was actually necessary for, one's genuine responsiveness to the needs and demands of others (Mill 1993, 70). Only once one had become a strong and self-confident individual would one be in a position to do genuine good for others, and only once one helped others insofar as it gave one more strength and joy could one be said to do so for the right reasons. Thus, "many actions called immoral ought to be avoided and resisted," and "many called moral ought to be done and encouraged–but for different reasons than formerly." The new reasons according to which an action ought to be done or resisted had to do with the degree to which it led to the flourishing of the self. But the way to attain the flourishing of the self, as the Ancients knew, was not by imposing one's will on the world in order to satisfy one's strongest desires at the expense of the needs and desires of others. Very often, the best way to help oneself was to help others.

This insight was at the root of Nietzsche's objection to the values embraced by Christian morality. It paralleled the troubles that many British thinkers had with the Comtian notion of altruism. Such values prescribed the reduction of self-interest in favor of the promotion of the good of others. They taught the value of charity and compassion, of bringing about good consequences for one's fellow sufferers. In Spencer's terms, it stressed altruism over egoism. But by taking the focus of one's ethical attention off the good of the self, and placing it instead on the good of others, this kind of value system too often resulted in personal corruption being papered over by superficial displays of charity. And even when Christian morality succeeded in reforming personal character, it did so only in order to make people nicer and more compassionate. But a society of compassionate and meek individuals would never amount to much. In Nietzsche's estimation, it would be far better for everyone, in the long run, if the compassionate man abandoned such feelings and acts, and focused instead on becoming the best possible version of himself. Those who did so, he thought, would be more inclined to genuine mercy and justice, and would be better equipped to effect real change.

What Nietzsche rejected, then, was the general Christian outlook that moral value was to be found in the complete reduction of self-interest, in meekness and humility, in self-sacrifice and a total regard for the good of all. Such values made sense in a Christian world, for they would ultimately be rewarded, either in this life or the next. To live a life dominated by the "ascetic ideal" – the ideal of abolishing one's own drives and desires – was to live a life closer to God. However, the death of God meant the loss of this promise. In a world without God, the meek would not inherit the earth. Rather, as the novelist Thomas Hardy pointed out – the very title of *Jude the Obscure* flags us to this – they were more likely to be ground down by the blind forces of fate. If one was to thrive in such a world, one would have to look after oneself first. In this new world, it would take a certain amount of vigor, a certain amount of guts, and ultimately a certain amount of self-interest to get ahead.

It seems, then, that we have come full circle. While Nietzsche criticized Eliot, Darwin, and Spencer for being too Christian, he ultimately came around to a position very similar to the one embraced by the likes of those Anglophones who, infused by evolutionary thought (or the ideas of progress that led to evolution), pointed to a new ethic, a new kind of morality. One who embodied this new morality would by no means be an amoral brute, but would possess a kind of vim and vigor not seen in New Testament conceptions of virtue. They were characters who sought their own interest, not merely at the blind expense of others, but because that is what is required to bring about a better world. Remember Thomas Henry Huxley.

Nietzsche as much as anyone was concerned with the project of bringing about a better world. Like the British evolutionists – no one respected the vigor and achievements of Huxley more than Charles Darwin – he saw that the providential picture of the world just didn't work anymore, which meant that our old morality, in some ways designed for this kind of world, had to be given up. In its place, we needed a new kind of morality, one better fit for the progressive world in which we lived. Yet it is important to stress that the kind of progress Nietzsche saw in the world was a characteristically German one. If the Anglophone post-*Origin* thinkers took their cue from the British industrial notion of progress, the new morality advocated by Nietzsche took its cue from the German notion of progress. It is here that we see the real difference between these thinkers emerge. Nietzsche's refusal to seek a new kind of morality in the theory of evolution was a function of his refusal to take seriously the Anglo-Saxon industrial ideal of progress. As he saw it, the very notion of Darwinian evolution was tainted by this picture of progress, which was ultimately the wrong one.

Nowhere was this clearer to Nietzsche than in Spencer's organicist depiction of the moral utopia waiting at the end of the process of evolution – and indeed serving as the final cause of that process. Spencer held that human nature was the product of a continuous process of the adaptation of inner, subjective states to the outer, objective social environment. This meant that over time, our individual social and psychological needs would come into a kind of harmony with the needs of others, resulting in the complete reconciliation of egoism and altruism. Due to the fact that pleasure was a product of successful adaptation and pain a product of maladaptation, the attainment of this kind of moral utopia would result in the maximization of pleasure for each individual (Spencer 1879). Evolution was guiding us inexorably to a social state in which there was no longer any tension between individuals, no longer any pain, no longer any struggle. It was guiding us to a society of perfect harmony, comfort, and peace. Whatever value Spencer attributed to strength, or to the survival of the fittest, was based on the idea that strength was a necessary means to the attainment of this moral ideal.

Nietzsche basically assumed that the same held true of the Darwinians generally. What these people really valued, he thought, was not so much the vim and vigor of individuals as the social and moral utopia that such individuals were supposed to help bring about, the utopia that evolution itself was gradually tending towards. This so-called utopia seemed more like a nightmare than an ideal to Nietzsche. He thought it would be a society of maximal conformity, marked by the loss of any kind of drive to individuality or ambition. In *Thus Spoke Zarathustra*, he described this kind of society as a society of "last men," totally content to wallow in their pleasurable state of harmony, rather than strive to become fully-fledged selves or to achieve anything great:

> What is love? What is creation? What is longing? What is a star? – thus asks the last man, blinking.
> Then the earth has become small, and on it hops the last man, who makes everything small. His kind is ineradicable, like the flea beetle; the last human being lives longest.
> 'We have invented happiness' – say the last human beings, blinking.
> They have abandoned the regions where it was hard to live: for one needs warmth. One still loves one's neighbor and rubs up against him: for one needs warmth. . . .
> . . . One still works, for work is a form of entertainment. But one sees to it that the entertainment is not a strain.
> One no longer becomes poor and rich: both are too burdensome. Who wants to rule anymore? Who wants to obey anymore? Both are too burdensome.
> No shepherd and one herd! Each wants the same, each is the same, and whoever feels differently goes voluntarily into the insane asylum . . .
> . . . 'We have invented happiness' say the last men, and they blink.
> (Nietzsche 2006, Zarathustra's Prologue §5)

The last men are stuck in a state of intellectual and moral stagnation, defined by widespread conformity and total apathy. This was not progress, but regress. If this was the state to which evolution was tending – and indeed Nietzsche thought it was – then evolution was the path to weakness and degeneration. It might well take guts to lead us forward on the path to this ideal, but at the end of the line there was nothing but feebleness and infirmity. (Shades of the *Time Machine!*)

Yet be not deceived that this is the end of the story. For Nietzsche too wanted progress. His obsession with overcoming Christian morality was a function of this desire. The problem with continuing with Christian values after the death of God was precisely the problem of degeneration. The great hope that a "revaluation" of values offered was the hope of progress, but progress of a distinctively German variety. It was not a matter of industrialization or the spread of equality and comfort; rather, it was a matter of the development and perfection of the spirit, which Nietzsche thought could only occur through unrelenting conflict and struggle. This view of progress is most commonly associated with Hegel, who saw history as "the development of spirit in time," which occurred through a series of conflicts between historical epochs, taking place at the level of ideas and leading ultimately to the absolute self-awareness of the World Spirit. This kind of progress – progress of Spirit – was importantly different from the kind that ruled in the world of Nature, which Hegel saw as in fact not progress at all, but rather "an eternally repeated cycle: "Thus Spirit, within its own self, stands in opposition to itself. It must overcome itself as its own truly hostile hindrance. The process of development, so quiescent in the world of nature, is for Spirit a hard and endless struggle against itself." (Hegel 1988, 58–59)

These ideas come up, in some way or another, in Nietzsche's works. Hence, Nietzsche's idea of progress was importantly distinct from the idea of progress as the Anglophone evolutionists saw it. For Nietzsche was concerned with progress of "the spirit," and this depended on overcoming the kind of social constitution that Spencer thought had been ingrained in us by nature (Richardson 2004, 162–171, 188). While Nietzsche rejected the world-historical, teleological aspect of the Hegelian notion of progress which claimed that historical movement was one of increasing rationalization, he still held, in a distinctively German manner, that the progress of thought and culture was all important, and that this progress required a certain amount of conflict and struggle to move from a less perfect state to a more perfect one. The ultimate goal was the cultivation of the individual mind (or spirit, or self), which demanded strength and the drive to overcome obstacles:

> For this goal one would need a different kind of spirits than are probable in this of all ages: spirits strengthened by wars and victories, for whom conquering, adventure, danger, pain have even become a need; for this one would need acclimatization to sharp high air, to wintry journeys, to ice and mountain ranges in every sense; for this one would need a kind of sublime malice itself, an ultimate most self-assured mischievousness of knowledge, which belongs

to great health; one would need, in brief and gravely enough, precisely this great health! (Nietzsche 1998, Treatise II §24)

And,

[I]f conflict and war affect such a nature as one more stimulus and goad to life –, and if genuine proficiency and finesse in waging war with himself (which is to say: the ability to control and outwit himself) are inherited and cultivated along with his most powerful and irreconcilable drives, then what emerge are those amazing, incomprehensible, and unthinkable ones, those human riddles destined for victory and seduction. (Nietzsche 1966, §200)

Nietzsche thought that this kind of conflict – which took place at the level of ideas – was fundamentally different from the evolutionary development which ruled in nature. Evolution, as he saw it, was not actually progressive at all; merely to follow its course would lead to a regressive society of last men. Real progress required the struggle of the spirit, and would lead to a society of strong, independent thinkers who sought above all to better themselves in the name of artistic and intellectual greatness. This would be progress in the true, German sense, not in the weak, British sense of "modern ideas," which, as he saw it, sought only increasing comfort, happiness, and luxury. But to bring it about required a shift in values, away from the ends of helping others and the reduction of suffering or the increase of pleasure, and towards the heroism of the individual pursuing the difficult task of developing her own thought, and thus contributing to the flourishing of culture.

So, like the Darwinians, Nietzsche recognized that the shift in worldview from a Christian perspective to a Darwinian one required a complementary shift in moral values from meekness to strength. This was never a matter of getting rid of morality altogether. It was a matter of recognizing that there is no reward waiting for the meek and humble, that if one wanted a better life one would have to roll up one's sleeves and work for it. In other words, it was ultimately a matter of progress. But unlike the Darwinians, Nietzsche thought that progress required continuous struggle to cultivate the spirit. Spencer's vision of a moral utopia characterized by complete self-sufficiency and perfect adaptation of inner relations to outer ones was anathema to Nietzsche, for he thought it would only ever result in a "stunted, almost ridiculous type, a herd animal, something well-meaning, sickly, and mediocre … the European of today" (Nietzsche 1966, §62). To the extent that "English Darwinism" saw the world as tending towards this state, Nietzsche held that it "[exuded] something like the stuffy air of English overpopulation, like the small people's smell of indigence and overcrowding" (Nietzsche 2001, §349).

To reaffirm: for Nietzsche, as much as for the Darwinians, it was a world "after Darwin." That was a shared perspective. What was not shared was the British notion of progress. This had no role to play in Nietzsche's Germanic-progressivist view of life. See the contrast. For the British, Thomas Henry Huxley was the exemplar of the good person – vigor and intelligence and through this contributing to the new world of commerce and industry, of science and technology, giving a better life for many people. For Nietzsche, to the contrary, the good person will be someone contributing to the spirit, to ideas, to culture. The poet Goethe is the epitome. "Goethe conceived of a strong, highly cultured human being, skilled in all physical accomplishments, who, keeping himself in check and having reverence for himself, dares to allow himself the whole compass and wealth of naturalness, who is strong enough for this freedom, a man of tolerance, not out of weakness, but out of strength, because he knows how to employ to his advantage what would destroy an average nature; a man to whom nothing is forbidden, except weakness, whether that weakness be called vice or virtue ... " (1954, *Expeditions* §49).

11 The Hitler Problem

Let us agree that the battle over social Darwinism seems to be a tie. Some truly dreadful things have been said and done in the name – or if not the name, the notion – of social Darwinism. There have also been enlightened views and actions in the name of the philosophy. And while some of the bad reputation has been truly earned, at times the movement has been somewhat unlucky as external events have occurred and impinged. So what about Hitler? Some scholars, such as the historian Richard Weikart (2004), lay the guilt at the feet of Darwin. Others, like the historian/philosopher Robert J Richards (2013), ardently deny the link. To be honest, if you look at Hitler – that is, if you look at *Mein Kampf* – the story seems dire.

> All great cultures of the past perished only because the originally creative race died out from blood poisoning.
>
> The ultimate cause of such a decline was their forgetting that all culture depends on men and not conversely; hence that to preserve a certain culture the man who creates it must be preserved. This preservation is bound up with the rigid law of necessity and the right to victory of the best and stronger in this world.
>
> Those who want to live, let them fight, and those who do not want to fight in this world of eternal struggle do not deserve to live. (Hitler 1925, 1, chapter 11)

Goodness! Apparently, that mild old scientist laboring away in the English countryside, not only provided the philosophy that led to the First World War, he did the same for the Second too! No wonder the critic can say: "The Darwinian underpinnings of Nazi racial ideology are patently obvious. Hitler's chapter on "Nation and Race" in Mein Kampf discusses the racial struggle for existence in clear Darwinian terms."[8] Before we leave the matter there, dig back a bit. In the context of material covered already in this Element, it seems that Hitler is simply carrying on the philosophy of people like von Bernhardi. Even if he is, however, the Darwin link is not established. It does not take long to realize that Friedrich von Bernhardi's ideas owe more to German idealism than to British industrialism. Going back to Hegel, for all of his idealism, and while there is much debate about Hegel's exact position on war, he certainly saw its upside. For Hegel and successors, not only was war a necessary and inevitable thing, in respects it was a good thing for us morally. It was not that he welcomed violence in itself – in fact, as with just war theory, Hegel demanded strong restrictions about not harming civilians – but he saw war as a necessary component in defining or delimiting one state from another. In context, particularly as we are building the best kind of state— as manifested by the growth and coming together of the parts to make the new Prussian-infused Germany. "I have remarked elsewhere, 'the ethical health of peoples is preserved in their indiffer-ence to the stabilisation of finite institutions; just as the blowing of the winds preserves the sea from the foulness which would be the result of a prolonged calm, so also corruption in nations would be the product of prolonged, let alone "perpetual" peace'" (Hegel 1821, 324; notice the jab at Kant).

　　Others sang the same song. Thus the philosopher Fichte. "The noble-minded man's belief in the eternal continuance of his influence even on this earth is thus founded on the hope of the eternal continuance of the people from which he has developed . . .. Hence, the noble-minded man will be active and effective, and will sacrifice himself for his people" (Fichte 1808, 115). As opposed to the kind of thinking we find in Darwin, although admittedly more in the Germanic-influenced Spencer, the value of the group over the individual is prominent. "Life merely as such, the mere continuance of changing existence, has in any case never had any value for him; he has wished for it only as the source of what is permanent. But this permanence is promised to him only by the continuous and independent existence of his nation. In order to save his nation, he must be ready even to die that it may live, and that he may live in it the only life for which he has ever wished" (Fichte 1821, 136).

　　The legacy of the holistic thinking of Hegel and others, whether or not it was always strictly what Hegel and others intended – in his convoluted way, Hegel

---

[8] Richard Weikart, "Was It Immoral for "Expelled" to Connect Darwinism and Nazi Racism?" (www.discovery.org/a/5069)

was far from a simple "might is right" philosophy – was supported and magnified by other forces, particularly the Volkish movement turning to a glorious (albeit fanciful) medieval past, captured and romanticized by the fairy tales collected by the Grimm brothers and, above all, by the operas of Wagner, with their epic stories of humans and gods in a now vanished world. We have a vision of the state as an organic unity, represented above all by the German state (Harrington 1996). Think of Hans Sachs' concluding sentiments (Act 3, Scene 5) of *Die Meistersinger*:

> Beware! Evil tricks threaten us; if the German people and kingdom should one day decay, under a false, foreign rule, soon no prince would understand his people; and foreign mists with foreign vanities they would plant in our German land; what is German and true none would know, if it did not live in the honour of German masters. Therefore, I say to you: honour your German masters, then you will conjure up good spirits! And if you favour their endeavors, even if the Holy Roman Empire should dissolve in mist, for us there would yet remain holy German Art!

Expectedly, given this sort of myth-making, as the nineteenth-century wended its way towards its end, German thinkers, especially those associated with the all-powerful military, gleaned supposedly supportive aspects of Darwin's thinking and, ignoring (as one is wont to do) the less supportive, found reasons to promote their own view of things. As with von Bernhardi, they were fanatically pro-German and thoroughly anti-British, a view not obviously found in the pages of the *Origin* or the *Descent*. Note the group thinking. "In the extrasocial struggle, in war, that nation will conquer which can throw into the scale the greatest physical, mental, moral, material, and political power, and is therefore the best able to defend itself." There is progress, yes, but not British industrial progress. Rather the progress of German idealism. Nietzsche did not come from nowhere.

German militarists were really using Darwin as cosmetic covering of home-grown philosophies dating back to the beginning of the nineteenth century or earlier. The same is true of Hitler. He was in the same tradition as the militarists, pushing German expansionism based on ideas of nineteenth-century German theorists. With his own agenda. Expansionism, building a future Germany without – Barbarossa – with a cleansing of past and present Germany within – the Final Solution. Hitler was not, to put it politely, a deeply well-read man (Kershaw 1999, 2000). Most of his thinking was picked up from the doss houses of Vienna before the First World War. In the passage quoted, really what he is talking about are the Jews. They must be wiped out for societal success. While one can certainly finger Luther and his anti-Semitism for this kind of thinking, neither Darwin nor Spencer give grounds for such an attitude (Richards 2013).

There are barely more than five or six mentions of Jews in Darwin's published writings and his total correspondence. When they do come up, it is usually in discussions of the evidential relevance of circumcision for Lamarckism. Darwin, in the *Descent*, is about as far from anticipating National Socialism as anyone could be. "The singular fact that Europeans and Hindoos, who belong to the same Aryan stock and speak a language fundamentally the same, differ widely in appearance, whilst Europeans differ but little from Jews, who belong to the Semitic stock and speak quite another language, has been accounted for by Broca through the Aryan branches having been largely crossed during their wide diffusion by various indigenous tribes" (1, 240). The most important German evolutionist between Darwin and Hitler was Ernst Haeckel. He went so far as to put the evolution of Jews on the same level as that of Aryans. Having opposed the First World War, he was no favorite of Hitler. Haeckel's works were removed from public libraries during the Third Reich (Richards 2008).

Going the other way, we have abundant evidence of the real sources of Hitler's anti-Semitism. When he was in Vienna, the mayor was the notorious Jew-hater Karl Lueger. In *Mein Kampf*, Hitler said explicitly that it was Lueger who set him on the road of anti-Semitism. Then, there was the influence of the English-born, Houston Stewart Chamberlain. A fanatical Wagnerian – he married the composer's daughter – his *Foundations of the Nineteenth Century* (1899) portrayed recent history as a battle between Aryans – "great, heavenly radiant eyes, golden hair, the body of a giant, harmonious musculature" and so forth – and the Jew – "materialistic, legalistic, limited in imagination, intolerant, fanatical, and with a tendency toward utopian economic schemes" (Richards 2013, 214–15). You get the idea. Hitler did. Chamberlain became Hitler's devoted admirer, and Hitler returned the favor, explicitly making heavy use of Chamberlain's thinking in *Mein Kampf*.

Finally, if more proof is needed of the non-relevance of Darwin for Hitler's thinking, one has the surely pertinent fact that Chamberlain did not believe in evolution, referring to Darwin's theory as akin to the discredited phlogiston theory. In this, he was followed by his disciple. Hitler did not believe in evolution either, certainly not in human evolution! In his *Table Talk*, recorded from conversations during the Second World War, he is persistent. "Whence have we the right to believe that man was not from the very beginning [Uranfängen] what he is today? A glance at nature informs us that in the realm of plants and animals alterations and further formation occur, but nothing indicates that development [Entwicklung] within a species [Gattung] has occurred of a considerable leap of the sort that man would have to have made to transform him from an apelike condition to his present state" (Richards 2013, 221). Enough said!

Or – not quite enough. Agree that people like von Bernhardi were, at best, using Darwinian theory as a gloss to give authenticity to what they were going to believe anyway. Agree that Hitler had his own agenda and Darwinism impinged, if at all, but little. However, Germanic worries about (an evolution-based) "racial hygiene" predate the First World War, with the newly developing discipline of criminology creating fears about the bad effects of breeding by lawbreakers. Add other factors, for instance that by the 1930s, with the fusion of Darwinian selection and Mendelian genetics, Darwinism – or Neo-Darwinism – was well on the way to becoming a well-established part of the scientific spectrum. It would be very unlikely that none of this would make its way to Germany, a country with – for all the perversions of the Third Reich – a deep and honorable scientific tradition. It would consequently be rash indeed to expect that no National Socialists would have any grasp of selection theory, which they could then use for their own ends. Such premonition proves to be true. Not very consistently, given his views on evolution, Hitler got into the act, this time following the turn-of-the-century criminologists in worrying about the ways in which the good are getting eliminated and the bad allowed to thrive and reproduce. "Every war leads to a negative selection. The positive elements die in masses. The choice of the most dangerous military service is already a selection: the really brave ones become airmen, or join the U-boats." Adding that "it is always the best men who then get killed. Conversely, "the absolute ne'er-do-well is cared for lovingly in body and spirit. Anyone who ever enters a prison knows with absolute certainty that nothing more is going to happen to him" (Evans 1997). These worries led to a horrendous increase in the use of capital punishment for even the most trivial of offences.

No Jews this time, but others were prepared to put selection theory to this end. Even by the standards of the Third Reich, the Wannsee Conference of 1942, on the outskirts of Berlin, where the "Final Solution" was discussed and agreed on, stands out as evil taken to lower depths than ever before. Right in the middle of the official minutes, the "Wannsee Protocol" – recorded by Adolf Eichmann – is Darwinian selection, invoked with proper understanding of its meaning and implications.[9] What is to happen to Europe's eleven million Jews? They are to be worked to death. If any survive then, because they are the fittest, they too must be killed off lest they parent a superior race.

> Under proper guidance, in the course of the final solution the Jews are to be allocated for appropriate labor in the East. Able-bodied Jews, separated according to sex, will be taken in large work columns to these areas for

---

[9] www.jewishvirtuallibrary.org/the-wannsee-protocol

work on roads, in the course of which action doubtless a large portion will be eliminated by natural causes.

The possible final remnant will, since it will undoubtedly consist of the most resistant portion, have to be treated accordingly, because it is the product of natural selection and would, if released, act as the seed of a new Jewish revival. (See the experience of history.)

12 Scientific Responsibility

The critics seem to have a point. How do we respond? Note that here the questions are more philosophical than historical. We know what happened. It is a matter of judging what happened. Is Charles Darwin culpable? Let's start with the truism that a mathematical or scientific statement as such has no value content. 2+2=4. The Earth goes around the Sun. Let's continue with the truism that scientists can have value commitments and that these can influence the science that they produce. Someone working on global warming may come up with findings about extinction that are in themselves value-free but that are discovered only because the scientists directed their labors in that direction rather than some other. Let us add another truism that sometimes the scientists' motives leave something to be desired. Working on the Manhattan project, for instance, making the atomic bomb. It is true that most of the scientists thought the bomb would be dropped on Germany. Many, though, didn't really think about it. They loved the project because the science and technology was "sweet" – tough, but in the realm of the possible, and then actual. Some, after the war, felt huge guilt. Some, like their president Harry Truman, did not. Either way, the science as produced was in a context hardly value-free.[10] The same sorts of issues came up in the 1970s, with the discovery of recombinant DNA techniques (Stitch 1978). This opened the way for the manufacture of very dangerous substances for very little monetary outlay. This time the scientists were on top of the problem and quickly put into place very careful state-enforced guidelines for such work. Yet another example is GMO technology and the moral issues surrounding it. In this case, controversy is ongoing. There is not the quick resolution of rDNA.

How far can one take the responsibility? If a nineteenth-century pure mathematician makes a discovery that in the twentieth century aids unpleasant actions and results – new weapons for instance – does one hold the mathematician morally culpable? Most would say not. What about Galileo? He discovered laws of motion that could be used for ballistics – the paths of cannon

---

[10] The movie, *The Day After Trinity*," about the making of the Bomb and the reactions later, is absolutely compulsive viewing.

balls given initial velocity and angle and so forth. He was supported by weaponry manufacturers. Was he culpable? Not so easy to say, especially given that often the only way one can do research is with the support of those with agendas. Even if we criticize Galileo for the Thirty Years War, do we still criticize him for the Battle of Jutland in 1916? Surely not, even though the laws were used in designing the battleships involved in the conflict. Or if not Galileo, then what about Euclid? Anyone who says he was responsible for teaching the Nazis geometry is not taking the argument seriously. No research could be done under such judgments. Conversely, the scientists in North Korea busy building bigger and better A-Bombs do have responsibility. It is all a question of making judgments between extremes. (See Brown 2013 for a more theoretical discussion of these points.)

These judgments tend to be more fraught over sciences that plunge us at once into questions about human beings. Someone, say, exploring the nature of plate tectonics is going to be less troubled than someone using human DNA to explore heritable traits. Darwinism doesn't have to be about human beings – it has as much relevance to warthog physiology and behavior. However, as we have seen, from the first it has been in the thick of discussions about our own species. This is not just incidental. Remember how Darwin's first speculations about natural selection were in the context of human thought and behavior. This has nothing to do with the status of the science itself. We would defend to the death the claim that Darwinism is genuine science, no less than the science of physics and chemistry. One of us stood up in federal court to defend this truth (Ruse 1988a).[11] However, let us not pretend that it is pure chance that it is Darwinian evolutionary theory that is the focus of our inquiry. And let us not pretend that Darwinians themselves have not been, in part, responsible for this state of affairs. The Nazi case quite apart, from Thomas Henry Huxley to Richard Dawkins there has been a tendency to convert Darwinian theory into a kind of secular religious alternative to Christianity – origins, humans, morality, sex, sin, and salvation (Ruse 2005, 2017a, 2018). It would have been remarkable, given their search for justifications of their appalling philosophy, had the National Socialists not mined Darwinian evolutionary theory to this end.

In the case of Hitler, one might say that he was so ignorant and messed up, it is hard to trace any real links in his case. Luther perhaps. Darwin less so. But

---

[11] This is not to say the methodologies of the physical sciences and the biological – including evolutionary – sciences are identical. There is reason to believe that the biological sciences recognize teleology in a way that the physical sciences do not (Ruse 2018b). This occurs simply because organisms are organized – functional – and inanimate objects are not. This does not imply that the biological sciences are inferior to the physical sciences. Just different. They could not do their job without their own ways of thinking.

the Wannsee Protocol seems like the proverbial smoking gun. Certainly, one cannot try the dodge that the science was being used inappropriately. Of course, inappropriately from a moral standpoint. But used as science, it seems legitimate. Moreover, for all that Darwin never would have used his theory to wipe out the Jews, the fact is that he was aware of the kinds of uses to which his theory could be put. The *Descent of Man* started the tradition of worrying about the bad effects of unrestrained breeding. "With savages, the weak in body or mind are soon eliminated; and those that survive commonly exhibit a vigorous state of health. We civilised men, on the other hand, do our utmost to check the process of elimination; we build asylums for the imbecile, the maimed, and the sick; we institute poor-laws; and our medical men exert their utmost skill to save the life of every one to the last moment" (Darwin 1871, 1, 168). This all comes about because we are nice people. "Nor could we check our sympathy, if so urged by hard reason, without deterioration in the noblest part of our nature." Unfortunately, not everyone's nature proved as noble as that of Charles Darwin and one might argue that he should have realized that. A counter argument is that one does realize that but senses a moral obligation to keep going with the work so one is always one step ahead of would-be malefactors.

So, we are at crunch time. It was Darwin's work – not Herbert Spencer's or anyone else – that was used by the Nazis in scientifically proper ways. As philosophers, we recognize that it is legitimate for us in the present to make moral judgments about people in the past. The American South was wrong about slavery. The Germans were wrong about Jews. (And conversely those who stood against the majority, like Sophie Scholl of the White Rose group, deserve moral praise.) We praise Darwin for his anti-slavery views. Why should we not therefore criticize him for his views on women, especially since there were contemporaries like John Stuart Mill who were challenging these societal assumptions? And, if women, why should we not criticize him for the Nazi use of his work? Simply because the arguments are not well taken. The women-Jew analogy is thin to the point of nonexistence. There are reasons to think that Darwin might have been more sensitive about women. There is absolutely no reason why Darwin – with no anti-Semitism in his record – should have anticipated Hitler and his crew. If Woodrow Wilson, David Lloyd George and all the other leaders in Versailles in 1919, after the Great War, clearly did not anticipate the Third Reich, why should Darwin be picked out for responsibility and guilt?

Even if Darwin had never existed, by 1941 the science would have been around for the Nazis to use. After all, Alfred Russel Wallace discovered the ideas in 1858 and Herbert Spencer nearly ten years before that. It would be ludicrous to finger Wallace for Auschwitz.[12] From its earliest days, natural selection was always at least the default position. By the 1920s and 1930s, it was common currency, however you regarded Darwin's overall theory and its applicability. A bit like Adam Smith. Everyone knows, or "knows," that a division of labor makes for efficiency. There is a tendency, a function of the arguments of people like Peter Bowler (1988) who deny the influence of natural selection, to think that Darwin's theory was just one among many. Hence, that someone would pick up on natural selection seems to need special justification. This premise is simply not well-taken (Ruse 2017a). Everybody knew about natural selection. No justification is needed for the use that even the Nazis made of Darwin's ideas.

In any case, the real worry is less about the mechanism of natural selection and more about evolution itself. The best-selling book, *Sapiens, A Brief History of Humankind*, by the Israeli author Yuval Noah Harari, identifies "evolutionary humanism" as the vile philosophy-cum-science behind Nazi ideology. He cites favorable Nazi references to natural selection as justification for his claim that Nazi views on *Untermenschen* come straight out of the evolutionary stew. But, apart from the fact that the Nazi beliefs about the inferiority of the Jews come from other non-evolutionary sources, apart from the fact that Hitler did not believe in evolution and the very linking of Aryans and Jews on the tree of life was suspect, belief in natural selection does not imply belief in evolution. Today, there are few more enthusiastic about natural selection than the Biblical Young Earth Creationists, who think that it all started six thousand years ago and took but six days. Both the Creationist Museum in Northern Kentucky and the Field Museum of Natural History in Chicago carry displays and discussions of natural selection. The one in the Creationist Museum is as good as if not better than the one in the Field Museum! This is not a one-off freak. On a Creationist webpage we learn: "Natural selection is considered to be the survival of the fittest and is often confused with evolution. But far from being proof for evolution and against creationism, natural selection is quite a reasonable and "God-given" process whereby we observe a certain genotype (the genetic makeup of an organism or group of organisms) that has pre-existed and has gradually adapted to one particular environment."[13] Richard Dawkins could not say it better, although one doubts he would cite Job in support "But ask the beasts, and they will teach you; the birds of the heavens, and they will

---

[12] Sometimes we encounter converse situations. Henry Clay Frick was one of the worst robber barons of the late nineteenth century. His role in the Homestead Strike has been noted. His donated art, The Frick Collection, is one of the jewels of New York City. Is it morally suspect to visit and admire the stunning Vermeer painting, "Mistress and Maid"?

[13] www.gotquestions.org/natural-selection.html

tell you; or the bushes of the earth, and they will teach you; and the fish of the sea will declare to you. Who among all these does not know that the hand of the Lord has done this?" (Job 12: 5–7).

What on earth is going on here? Simply that the Creationists realize that the Ark would have been unable to carry all the species of animal living today. The argument is that the Ark carried "types" or "kinds" that then, the Flood over, diversified into the species we see today. And the force behind all of this? Natural selection. The Galapagos finches are as important to the Creationists as they are to the Darwinians, implying that, if your worry is evolution and its supposed implications about Jews, don't blame Darwinian selection. And with this point made, enough really has been said.[14]

13 Echoes of The Past

Although no one calls it that, today, social Darwinism thrives, and if not always in quite the best quarters – the hallowed halls of the analytic philosophy that dominates today in Anglo-American circles – in ways quite adequate for its (enthusiastic) supporters. It is true that, until at least the 1960s, the chill of *Principia Ethica* brought shivers of fright to one and all. The older of the authors remembers his introduction to philosophy at the beginning of that decade. To doubt the naturalistic fallacy would have been on a par with doubting the virginity of Mary in Medieval Europe. This does not mean that there had been no attempt to resuscitate a form of Spencerian ethics. Although Thomas Henry Huxley had little time for Spencerian-type thinking, his biologist grandson Julian Huxley was an enthusiast. He was an ardent progressionist, thinking that as we go up the scale, value increases – things get better. "When we look at evolution as a whole, we find, among the many directions which it has taken, one which is characterized by introducing the evolving world-stuff to progressively higher levels of organization and so to new possibilities of being, action, and experience" (Huxley 1943b, 41–42). A scientist, writing during the 1930s and 1940s, Julian Huxley thought – not surprisingly – that (particularly at the societal level) we should be promoting the virtues and benefits of science and technology. Responding to the Great Recession, we find that Huxley was a great enthusiast for the public works funded by Franklin Roosevelt's New Deal. Although stepping somewhat warily because he did not want to be seen as

---

[14] This is not to say that the Creationists are happy with the evolutionary ends to which Darwin put natural selection. Their animus is not against Darwin as a person, but against the theory he discovered and embellished. Disputing this, first the critics tried to counter Darwin and his theory scientifically. That failed (Gilkey 1985; Ruse 1988a). Then they tried to counter Darwin and his theory philosophically. That failed (Pennock 1998; Forrest and Gross 2004; Lebo 2008). Now they try to counter Darwin morally. This fails too.

endorsing the war preparations of the National Socialists – the building of the Autobahn for example – Huxley was fairly unrestrained in his encomia for the Tennessee Valley Authority, that project bringing electricity to large parts of the American South (Huxley 1943a). After the Second World War, Huxley became the first director general of UNESCO. It was he who insisted that the United Nations go beyond just education and culture to include science also. He wrote a little book praising progress and declaring it the philosophy of the new organization (Huxley 1948). His overseers were so shocked, they cut his intended term from four years to two. It is no surprise either that the philosopher C. D. Broad, student of G. E. Moore, should react negatively to all of this. He could not see whether evolution "has any direct bearing on the question whether certain states of affairs or processes or experiences would be intrinsically good or bad" (Broad 1944, 363). *Principia Ethica* all over again.

Whether the philosophers' criticisms had any real effect, overall, social Darwinism, however called, was basically on hold for the first half of the twentieth century, at least for the half after the Great War. Optimistic philosophies of progress seemed almost indecent. Then things changed. The key factor bringing on a change of attitude was the development in the 1960s and 1970s of a properly articulated theory of the evolution of social behavior, in animals and in humans. Darwin himself had discussed social behavior in the *Origin* – the social insects in particular – but for a century after, with the notable exception of the Continental ethologists, it languished. This was partly because of the difficulties of studying behavior – it is much easier to study morphology if you have the dead organism on your dissecting table – and partly because of the rise of the social sciences, whose insecurities made them hostile to any biological explanations of behavior. You've seen one white rat; you've seen them all. Countering such simplistic thinking, by the one hundredth anniversary of the *Origin* (1959), new models that explain social behavior were being devised. Mechanisms such as kin selection and reciprocal altruism were articulated and increasingly found to have empirical support. Before long, that key factor in human behavior – morality – was bound to come under the gaze of these new "sociobiologists" (Ruse 1979b).

Hugely important was the 1975 publication of the Harvard ant specialist, Edward O. Wilson: *Sociobiology: The New Synthesis*. Intentionally paying homage to Julian Huxley's massive 1942 overview of then-contemporary evolutionary theory, *Evolution: The Modern Synthesis*, Wilson offers a like, massive overview of his field, starting with mechanisms and then going on to a huge survey of animal social behavior, from the most primitive forms up to and including our own species, *Homo sapiens*. At once, there was (perhaps expected) opposition from social scientists, and (perhaps unexpected) opposition from fellow evolutionary biologists. The former were frightened of being put out of jobs and the latter were upset because Wilson was taken to challenge Marxist commitments. Additionally, some felt that taking a biological approach to humankind was redolent of Third Reich attitudes to humankind (Segerstrale 1986).

Whatever the full story, the evolution of human social behavior was out on the table, and that meant morality. Wilson welcomed this fact. In *Sociobiology: The New Synthesis*, firmly he put ethics at the front of his endeavors. If the title of the first chapter, "The morality of the gene", does not flag you, then the opening words surely will:

> Camus said that the only serious philosophical question is suicide. That is wrong even in the strict sense intended. The biologist, who is concerned with questions of physiology and evolutionary history, realizes that self-knowledge is constrained and shaped by the emotional control centers in the hypothalamus and limbic systems of the brain. These centers flood our consciousness with all the emotions – hate, love, guilt, fear, and others – that are consulted by ethical philosophers who wish to intuit the standards of good and evil. What, we are then compelled to ask, made the hypothalamus and limbic system? They evolved by natural selection. That simple biological statement must be pursued to explain ethics and ethical philosophers, if not epistemology and epistemologists, at all depths. (Wilson 1975, 3)

That upset the philosophers, something Wilson felt able to bear with equanimity. It helped that, rather than a reasoned philosophical strategy, Wilson had more of a gut feeling about how to go forward. We must put things in context. In this Element, we have seen two options – two ways in which one might relate evolutionary biology to moral understanding. Acknowledging that Darwin shared the prejudices of his tribe, we can continue to call these the Darwinian approach and the Spencerian approach. The former, the Darwinian approach, argues that there are no metaethical foundations to normative ethics, and that hence one is forced to be a moral non-realist. This does not mean that one is at once a traditional social Darwinian of the most selfish and repellant kind. It does argue, for it is Darwin's theory of evolution (and not evolution generally) that is at its core, that morality is a very human thing. An adaptation. The latter, the Spencerian approach, is by far the more popular. Closer to traditional social Darwinism, but still a way apart, the key assumption – the metaethical foundation of its normative ethics – is progress. Things are getting better and our moral obligations are to keep this process going. Whereas the first position is metaethically subjective, this position is metaethically objective. It would still be true even if there were no one around in the forest. You have turned to the dictates of nature rather than the dictates of God.

Wilson is the paradigm, the Platonic Form, of the second approach.[15] Sociobiology may have been new, but at heart Wilson is a nineteenth-century, unreconstructed Spencerian (Ruse 2013). He may have paid homage to Charles Darwin, but his heritage was Spencerian. The supervisor of Wilson's supervisor was the ant specialist William Morton Wheeler (Evans and Evans 1970). Enthusiastically Spencerian, Wheeler drew significant parallels between human and ant societies. He thought of ant nests as the insect equivalent of individual organisms. "An ant society, therefore, may be regarded as little more than an expanded family, the members of which cooperate for the purpose of still further expanding the family and detaching portions of itself found other families of the same kind. There is thus a striking analogy, which has not escaped the philosophical biologist, between the ant colony and the cell colony which constitutes the body of a Metazoan animal . . ." Adding that the "queen mother of the ant colony displays the generalized potentialities of all the individuals, just as a Metazoan egg contains in potentia all the other cells of the body. And continuing the analogy, we may say that since the different castes of the ant colony are morphologically specialized for the performance of different functions, they are truly comparable with the differentiated tissues of the Metazoan body" (Wheeler 1910, 7). Take note of the Spencerian holism. It is the group rather than the individual ant that is the unit of selection. There is a break here with Darwin, who thought the individual ants are the units, and make up a super-organism through self-interest.

Wilson buys into all of this, not the least in upsetting a good 95% of his fellow evolutionists by arguing strongly for the holistic group selection over the reductionistic individual selection (Wilson and Wilson 2007). Expectedly, also, Wilson is an ardent progressionist, with his ordering of organisms in *Sociobiology* from the simplest to the most complex, from "monad to man," as they used to say in earlier times. "Man has intensified these vertebrate traits while adding unique qualities of his own. In so doing he has achieved an extraordinary degree of cooperation with little or no sacrifice of personal survival and reproduction." The big question is not whether progress occurred, but why it occurred. "Exactly how he alone has been able to cross to this fourth pinnacle, reversing the downward trend of social evolution in general, is the culminating mystery of all biology" (Wilson 1975, 382). In later works, Wilson expands on this. "The overall average across the history of life has moved from the simple and few to the more complex and numerous. During the past billion years, animals as a whole evolved upward in body size, feeding and defensive

---

[15] Assuming that is that one can have Platonic Forms of anything Spencerian. In the *Parmenides*, Plato queried whether one can have Platonic Forms of hair, mud, and dirt.

techniques, brain and behavioral complexity, social organization, and precision of environmental control – in each case farther from the nonliving state than their simpler antecedents did" (Wilson 1992, 187). Adding: "Progress, then, is a property of the evolution of life as a whole by almost any conceivable intuitive standard, including the acquisition of goals and intentions in the behavior of animals."

Totally indifferent to the naturalistic fallacy – it may apply in some instances but not here – Wilson moves on to social issues. As Julian Huxley's prescriptions reflected the challenges of his era, so Edward O. Wilson's prescriptions reflect the challenges of our era. Expectedly, as one whose naturalist callings took him to exotic places like the Brazilian rain forests, Wilson has concern about the environment, specifically about biodiversity (Wilson 1984, 1992, 2012). He worries a great deal about the ways in which modern society is destroying the natural habitat and how with this comes the subsequent decline of natural resources and species diversity. Wilson sees humans as having evolved in symbiotic relationship with nature. Apart from the utilitarian factors – how for instance unknown, exotic species might produce substances of great social and medical benefit – Wilson believes, in an almost aesthetic way, that humans need the growing living world. An environment of plastic would kill, literally as well as metaphorically. In *The Future of Life*, Wilson declares: "a sense of genetic unity, kinship, and deep history are among the values that bond us to the living environment. They are survival mechanisms for us and our species. To conserve biological diversity is an investment in immortality" (Wilson 2002, 133).

Wilson might be dismissed as a one-off. As noted, that was the immediate reaction of philosophers. Satisfyingly, his follow-up book, exclusively on our species, *On Human Nature*, won Wilson the first of his Pulitzer Prizes. However, by the middle of the next decade, the 1980s, more rational people – or more susceptible people, take your choice – were starting to rethink things. Thomas Henry Huxley had pointed out that we humans are modified monkeys, rather than modified mud, and that surely had to mean something. After all, to go back to G. E. Moore, he of the naturalistic fallacy, his position was hardly appealing. Apparently, morality is all a matter of non-natural properties, whatever they might be. The suspicion is that they might be like Platonic Forms, and Moore's own comments do not belie this suspicion. "I am pleased to believe that this is the most Platonic system of modern times" (Baldwin 1990, 50). Much as we admire Plato, having given up God, many of us would prefer not to have to put Plato's Form of the Good in His place. As we have seen, this "many" does not include most Anglophone philosophers of the twentieth century.

Thus, a forthright exposition of the Spencerian position. Let us not pause to criticize. Nothing we could say has not been said already about earlier writers of this persuasion. What now about an exposition of the Darwinian position? The older author has been arguing this for over thirty years, so look briefly at his arguments and conclusions (Ruse 1986a, b; Ruse and Richards 2017), as we will leave Wilson's Spencerian position to speak for itself, and we shall let Michael Ruse's position do the same. Which is right or better, or if neither are satisfactory, is a judgment, as they say, which is left to the reader. Fitness will out!

Ruse really is a Darwinian and not just an evolutionist. Like Darwin he thinks that cooperation can be a very successful adaptive strategy, and like Darwin he thinks it can be brought about by natural selection. Raised a Quaker, Ruse has long been a non-believer – agnostic rather than atheist – and sees no reason to appeal to God or to any other external standard or truth in explaining morality. He thinks we are nice to each other because it pays off, and he thinks that morality is a quick and dirty solution to the cooperation problem. Like Darwin he thinks that natural selection works only at the individual level – allowing that tribes are interrelated or that the members think they are – and that there is nothing sacred, non-naturalistic, about our moral sense. In theory, we could do away with morality and decide everything on a rational basis, rather as we do when we enter a store to go shopping. However, as Kant (1785) pointed out, this would be a clumsy way of doing things. Time is money and morality lets us get on with life. It may sometimes lead to bad adaptive decisions but that is the risk with quick and dirty solutions.

So much for the substantive level of discussion. Ruse is ecumenical about the content of the normative dictates. Probably a combination of utilitarianism and Kantianism – we ought to maximize happiness but we should not do it at the expense of individuals. As somewhat of a pragmatist – note that the Pragmatists were keen Darwinians – Ruse is not bothered that sometimes there are going to be difficult issues. Should you bribe a concentration camp warder to let a group of children escape? You are maximizing happiness but you are not treating him as an end in itself. Not believing in objective morality, there is no definitive answer. There are times when you must wing it by the seat of your pants. Few adaptations work perfectly all the time. Liking sweet things has obvious adaptive value, but equally there are times when liking sweet things is a rotten biological strategy. Same with moral rules.

John Rawls in his *Theory of Justice* appeals to Darwinism to explain why we think as we do, and this seems basically right.

> In arguing for the greater stability of the principles of justice I have assumed that certain psychological laws are true, or approximately so. I shall not

pursue the question of stability beyond this point. We may note however that one might ask how it is that human beings have acquired a nature described by these psychological principles. The theory of evolution would suggest that it is the outcome of natural selection; the capacity for a sense of justice and the moral feelings is an adaptation of mankind to its place in nature. (Rawls 1971, 502–503)

Rawls (1980) rushes to say that this does not justify things and Ruse would agree. However, whereas Rawls sets off to find Kantian justification for his position – necessary conditions for rational beings to interact socially – Ruse simply concludes that there is no justification, not of an objective kind, God, Plato, or Kant. Is this not too quick a move? You cannot simply appeal to the Darwinian origins of our moral sense. After all, if a truck is bearing down on us, we use Darwinian-evolved adaptations to get out of its way. The situation is different in the morality case. You must sense the truck or you die. You might not sense the real, true objective morality – and yet go through life happily in ignorance. Darwin pointed us this way with his example of the bees. Take a case closer to home: the moral system of John Foster Dulles, President Eisenhower's Secretary of State in the 1950s. He hated the Russians, they hated him. He thought he had a moral obligation to hate them, and conversely. But they got on just fine in the Cold War because they realized reciprocation is needed. So, in the end, everyone survived and reproduced. If this isn't a reductio of objective morality, Ruse doesn't know what would be. We could go through life functioning happily, with our own morality, totally ignorant of what the real morality is like. You just cannot go through life in ignorance of 2+2=4. At least you cannot go through life with an alternative mathematics – 2+2=5. Apparently, you can with morality! Of course, you can't, so moral non-realism seems to be the consequence.

Ask some questions. Is the normative morality going to be just like pre-*Origin* morality, Christianity for instance? Ruse agrees with the post-Darwinians that vigor and guts count. They really do! In 1980, to promote awareness of the need of cancer research, a twenty-two-year-old Canadian, Terry Fox, who had lost a leg to cancer, decided to run across Canada – from the Atlantic to the Pacific. By the time he got to Ontario, Terry had attracted huge attention and there was not a person in Canada who was not rooting for him. The story has a sad end, for his journey was unfinished before the cancer recurred and he died the next summer. No one – no one – doubted that what Terry was doing was something of great moral significance. This was not a young man who accepted his fate, meekly.

An interesting question is about the scope of morality. Christianity is somewhat fuzzy on this. The parable of the Good Samaritan suggests that we have equal moral obligations to every human. Jesus is rather nasty about those who mention family obligations. "If anyone comes to me and does not hate his own father and mother and wife and children and brothers and sisters, yes, and even his own life, he cannot be my disciple" (Luke 14:26). At other times, it is suggested strongly that you have special obligations to family members. "But if any provide not for his own, and specially for those of his own house, he hath denied the faith, and is worse than an infidel" (1 Timothy 5:8). The Darwinian ethicist is strongly committed to family first and most probably friends and acquaintances second. That does not mean you have no obligations to strangers – to give to Physicians without Borders – but that charity begins at home.

David Hume was, as so often, ahead of us all on this. "A man naturally loves his children better than his nephews, his nephews better than his cousins, his cousins better than strangers, where every thing else is equal. Hence arise our common measures of duty, in preferring the one to the other. Our sense of duty always follows the common and natural course of our passions" (Hume 1739–40, 483–484). You don't have to be a Darwinian to know that morally you feel this way – morally you should feel this way – it is not just personal feelings, like eating spinach. Charles Dickens knew the score. In *Bleak House* (1853), he is scathing about the philanthropist Mrs. Jellyby who spends her days raising funds for a tribe in Africa while at the same time she ignores the needs of her own family, let alone the poor of her nation – Jo, the crossing sweeper.

Remind ourselves why relativism is not an issue, at least only in a non-troublesome way. Perhaps on a planet, far, far away, as the saying goes, there are rational humanoids who are governed by Dulles' morality. Their morality is relative to their planet as ours is to ours. On our planet, there are clearly relative issues connected with culture – should women out of doors cover their heads or not? – but at the deeper biological level there is no relativism. There cannot be if morality is to work. Adolescent boys may have dreams of being endowed like the Brontosaurus, but truly, if they are not within limits, their reproductive careers are going to be as unproductive as if they were endowed like field mice. Someone who is super-moral or super-immoral will just not fit in. As will someone who has no or a different moral faculty. We call them psychopaths. (Does that mean we think Dulles was immoral? We suspect most of us avoid that question by arguing that Dulles was simply following game-theoretical rules, with no morality involved either way. This doesn't mean you couldn't have such a system infused with moral sentiments.)

Finally, are we not shooting ourselves in the moral foot? Having told you that morality is an illusion of the genes, why not go out and rape and pillage? There is no morality and so if you can get away with it, then go for it. Good question and there is a good answer. The difference between moral sentiments and other emotions and convictions and likes and dislikes is that part of the (for want of a better word) phenomenology of morality is that we think it more than the both of us – we "objectify" it. If one declares a passion for fish and chips with lots of salt and vinegar, one does not necessarily expect others to feel the same. You fall passionately in love. You would probably be upset if others could not see why one might fall in love with one's object of devotion. Probably, however, one is glad that others do not fall in love with the same object! However, if one makes a moral claim – thou shalt not mark up library books in yellow with a felt pen – one expects it to be binding on others. Morality may not be based on Platonic Forms, but it comes across as if it is. If it didn't, it wouldn't work. We would all start cheating and within a short while the moral system would collapse.

14 And The World Said?

The younger co-author of this Element asserts himself. Much as the older co-author would be happy to conclude with the brilliance of his position ringing in the reader's ears, this is not the intent of this Element. Inasmuch as we are historians, we are not directly concerned with questions of right or wrong. Our task is to lay out people's thinking on these matters. However, inasmuch as we are philosophers, our questions are different and do involve moral judgments. What is most striking about our story? Simply: *plus ça change, plus c'est la même chose.* We entered this Element with Darwin and Spencer. Their scientific theories, despite overlap, were different. For Spencer, progress, holism and moral realism were all important. For Darwin, progress was secondary and derived, and individualism and moral non-realism were both important. Yet, at another level, Darwin and Spencer had similar concerns. They were trying to articulate a post-Christian morality, and much that they said – about social issues – overlapped. Both saw the importance of effort and trying to succeed, both accepted many of the assumptions of their society, both hoped for the end of militarism. Yet at the same time, there were differences, reflecting Darwin's comfortable upper-middle-class status and Spencer's lower-middle-class resentments at the injustices that he felt burdened people such as he. Darwin was no socialist. Spencer could be read as one.

Wilson and Ruse are polar opposites. Scientifically, Wilson pushes the Spencerian line. He believes in progress, his commitment to group selection advertises his holism, and he thinks one can give a naturalistic foundation to moral claims. Ruse is not keen on progress, he is a fanatical individual selectionist, and he thinks morality can be given no objective foundation, natural or otherwise. There are social differences. Wilson is the product of the conservative American South of the years before, during, and after the Second World War – he thinks in terms of different sex roles – and he cares now about matters of biological importance, like the preservation of the Amazonian rainforests. He emphasizes group aspects of culture, for instance the importance of a shared religious commitment and practice. Ruse, English-born and raised, is the product of a more liberal and cosmopolitan social environment. For him, more pressing than the rainforests are social issues like sexual equality and gay rights. Revealingly, whereas Wilson has written about biodiversity, Ruse has written about homosexuality (Wilson 1992; Ruse 1988b). As revealingly, although both Wilson and Ruse are non-believers, Wilson who came from this culture, reaches out to evangelical Christians (Wilson 2006). Ruse, whose religion was very, very British in its distaste for enthusiasm, has spent forty years opposing evangelicals (Ruse 1988a, 2015, 2019). Truly, though, at this point the similarities are greater than the differences. Darwin, Spencer, Wilson, Ruse – none of them have much time for religious belief.

As in the nineteenth century, both Wilson and Ruse have been severely chastised for their moral thinking. As soon as *Sociobiology: The New Synthesis* hit the bookstores, a left-wing group, Science for the People, publicly denounced him. "In his attempt to graft speculation about human behavior onto a biological core, Wilson uses a number of strategies and sleights of hand which dispel any claim for logical or factual continuity." Whatever was said about the science paled beside the moral indignation. Although it truly was a case of *déjà vu* all over again. "These theories provided an important basis for the enactment of sterilization laws and restrictive immigration laws by the United States between 1910 and 1930 and also for the eugenics policies which led to the establishment of gas chambers in Nazi Germany" (Allen et al 1975). Ruse likewise has been the object of public moral scorn (Ruse 2017c, d, e). Typical was the response to Ruse's claim that we have differential moral sentiments, favoring family over nonrelatives, and fellow societal members over outsiders. "Social Darwinizing still creates safe niches for selfishness on planet Earth" (Moore 1986, 72).

Plus ça change, plus c'est la même chose! Are Wilson and Ruse playing the same game as the Victorians? And to the same end? It is not that the science is wrong, although, as with Darwin and Spencer, there are certainly irreconcilable differences in their respective positions. Nor is the morality always at fault. We should care about the rainforests. The real problem, charge the critics, is that, as with Darwin and Spencer, Wilson and Ruse are reading their moral beliefs into their science and then promptly fishing them out again as objective! "What we are left with then is a particular theory about human nature, which has no scientific support, and which upholds the concept of a world with social arrangements remarkably similar to the world which E. O. Wilson inhabits" (Allen et al 1975). The reasoning is circular. Perhaps Ruse is right that ultimately all action has to be judged in terms of personal gain, but this is a moral belief not a scientific belief. It may be that things only work in terms of personal gain. Remember Thomas Henry Huxley. It may well be that we humans have succeeded only because we have (or have had) tiger- and ape-like characteristics. This does not make them morally right or desirable. As which point Wilson and Ruse will make the obvious response. If there is circularity, it is not vicious circularity, but more a kind of reinforcing process that occurs frequently in the work of confirmation. You have moral belief A, say about the importance of self-effort. This leads you to formulate scientific theory B, that works through self-interest. If you leave matters there or simply use B to support A, you are indeed viciously circular. But if you go out and show empirically, independently, that B works, this is another matter. Now it is legitimate to return to A, where now you might refine your A to A', leading to B', and so forth. Nothing wrong here.

Enough. The younger co-author of this Element has made his point. And together we have made the more important point. Social Darwinism raises matters of considerable and timely philosophical interest.

Bibliography

Allen, E., and others. 1975. Letter to the editor. *New York Review of Books*, sec. 22, 18, pp. 43–44.

Baldwin, T. 1990. *G. E. Moore*. London: Routledge and Kegan Paul.

Balfour, A. 1895. *The Foundations of Belief*. New York: Longmans, Green.

Bannister, R. J. 1979. *Social Darwinism: Science and Myth in Anglo-American Social Thought*. Philadelphia: Temple University Press.

Bellamy, E. [1887] 1951. *Looking Backward, 2000–1898*. New York: Modern Library.

Bellomy, D. C. 1984. 'Social Darwinism' Revisited. *Perspectives in American History* n.s. 1: 1–129.

Bowler, P. J. 1988. *The non-Darwinian Revolution: Reinterpreting a Historical Myth*. Baltimore, Md.: Johns Hopkins University Press.

Broad, C. D. 1944. Critical notice of Julian Huxley's *Evolutionary Ethics*. *Mind* 53: 344–67.

Brown, M. J. 2013. Values in science beyond underdetermination and inductive risk. *Philosophy of Science* 80: 829–39.

Browne, J. 1995. *Charles Darwin: Voyaging. Volume 1 of a Biography*. London: Jonathan Cape.

2002. *Charles Darwin: The Power of Place. Volume 2 of a Biography*. London: Jonathan Cape.

Burton, D. H. 1965. Theodore Roosevelt's Social Darwinism and Views on Imperialism. *Journal of the History of Ideas* 26: 103–18.

Carnegie, A. 1889. The Gospel of Wealth. *North American Review* 148: 653–65.

Chamberlain, H. S. 1899. *Die Grundlagen des neunzehnten Jahrhunderts (Foundations of the Nineteenth Century)*. Munich: Bruckmann.

Chambers, R. 1846. *Vestiges of the Natural History of Creation*. 5th ed. London: J. Churchill.

Clark, M. 1994. Nietzsche's immoralism and the concept of morality. *Nietzsche, Genealogy, Morality: Essays on Nietzsche's Genealogy of Morals*. Editor R. Schacht Berkeley: University of California Press.

Common, T., Editor. 1901. *Nietzsche as Critic, Poet, and Prophet: Choice Selections from His Works*. New York: E. P. Dutton and Company.

Crook, P. 1994. *Darwinism, War and History: The Debate over the Biology of War from the 'Origin of Species' to the First World War*. Cambridge: Cambridge University Press.

Darwin, C. 1845. *Journal of Researches into the Natural History and Geology of the Countries Visited during the Voyage of H.M.S. Beagle round the World [2nd ed.]*. London: John Murray.

1859. *On the Origin of Species by Means of Natural Selection, or the Preservation of Favoured Races in the Struggle for Life*. London: John Murray.

1861. *Origin of Species, Third Edition*. London: John Murray.

1871. *The Descent of Man, and Selection in Relation to Sex*. London: John Murray.

1958. *The autobiography of Charles Darwin 1809–1882. With the original omissions restored. Edited and with appendix and notes by his granddaughter Nora Barlow*. London: Collins.

1985. *The Correspondence of Charles Darwin*. Cambridge: Cambridge University Press.

1987. *Charles Darwin's Notebooks, 1836–1844*. Editors P. Barrett, P. J. Gautrey, S. Herbert, D. Kohn, and S. Smith. Ithaca, N. Y.: Cornell University Press.

Desmond, A. 1998. *Huxley: From Devil's Disciple to Evolution's High Priest*. London: Penguin.

Dickens, C. [1853] 1948. *Bleak House*. Oxford: Oxford University Press.

1854 [1948]. *Hard Times*. Oxford: Oxford University Press.

1865 [1948]. *Our Mutual Friend*. Oxford: Oxford University Press.

Dixon, T. 2008. *The Invention of Altruism: Making Moral Meanings in Victorian Britain*. Oxford: Oxford University Press.

Evans, M. A., and H. E. Evans. 1970. *William Morton Wheeler, Biologist*. Cambridge, Mass.: Harvard University Press.

Evans, R. J. 1997. In Search of German Social Darwinism. *Rereading German Social History: From Unification to Reunification, 1800–1996*. Author and Editor R. J. Evans, 119–44. London: Routledge.

Fichte, J. G. 1821 [1922]. *Addresses to the German Nation*. Chicago: Open Court.

Fisher, J. 1877. A history of landholding in Ireland. *Transactions of the Royal Historical Society* 5: 228–326.

Forrest, B., and P. R. Gross. 2004. *Creationism's Trojan Horse: The Wedge of Intelligent Design*. Oxford: Oxford University Press.

Gladden, W. 1905. *Christianity and Socialism*. New York: Eaton and Mains.

Gilkey, L. B. 1985. *Creationism on Trial: Evolution and God at Little Rock*. Minneapolis: Winston Press.

Hamilton, W. D. 1964 a. The genetical evolution of social behaviour I. *Journal of Theoretical Biology* 7: 1–16.

1964 b. The genetical evolution of social behaviour II. *Journal of Theoretical Biology* 7: 17–32.

Harari, Y. N. 2015. *Sapiens: A Brief History of Humankind*. New York: Harper.

Hardy, T. [1895] 1960. *Jude the Obscure*. London: Macmillan.

Harrington, A. 1996. *Reenchanted Science: Holism in German Culture from Wilhelm II to Hitler*. Princeton, N. J.: Princeton University Press.

Hawkins, M. 1997. *Social Darwinism in European and American Thought 1860–1945*. Cambridge: Cambridge University Press.

Hegel, G. W. F. [1817] 1970. *Philosophy of Nature*. Oxford: Oxford University Press.

1988. *Introduction to the Philosophy of History*. Translator L. Rauch. Indianapolis: Hackett.

1991. *Elements of the Philosophy of Right*. Editor A. Wood. Cambridge: University of Cambridge Press.

Hitler, A. 1925 [1939]. *Mein Kampf*. London: Hurst & Blackett.

Hofstadter, R. 1944 [1992]. *Social Darwinism in American Thought [1860–1915]*. Boston: Beacon Press.

Hume, D. [1739–1740] 1978. *A Treatise of Human Nature*. Oxford: Oxford University Press.

[1757] 1963. A Natural History of Religion. *Hume on Religion*. Editor R. Wollheim. London: Fontana.

Huxley, J. S. 1942. *Evolution: The Modern Synthesis*. London: Allen and Unwin.

1943a. *TVA: Adventure in Planning*. London: Scientific Book Club.

1943b. *Evolutionary Ethics*. Oxford: Oxford University Press.

1948. *UNESCO: Its Purpose and Its Philosophy*. Washington, D.C.: Public Affairs Press.

Huxley, T. H. 1893. *Evolution and Ethics with a New Introduction*. Edited by M. Ruse. Princeton: Princeton University Press.

Jones, G. 1980. *Social Darwinism and English Thought*. Brighton: Harvester.

Kant, I. [1785]1959. *Foundations of the Metaphysics of Morals*. Indianapolis: Bobbs-Merrill.

[1795]1970. Perpetual peace: a philosophical sketch. *Kant: Political Writings*. I. Kant, 93–130. Cambridge: Cambridge University Press.

Kellogg, V. L. 1905. *Darwinism Today*. New York: Henry Holt.

1917. *Headquarters Nights: A Record of Conversations and Experiences at the Headquarters of the German Army in France and Belgium*. Boston: Atlantic Monthly Press.

Kershaw, I. 1999. *Hitler 1889–1936: Hubris*. New York: Norton.

2000. *Hitler, 1936–1945: Nemesis*. New York: Norton.

Kropotkin, P. 1902. *Mutual Aid: A Factor in Evolution*. Boston: Extending Horizons Books.

Lankester, E. R. 1880. *Degeneration: A Chapter in Darwinism*. London: Macmillan.

Lebo, L. 2008. *The Devil in Dover: An Insider's Story of Dogma v. Darwin in Small-Town America*. New York: New Press.

Leonard, T. C. 2009. Origins of the Myth of Social Darwinism: The Ambiguous Legacy of Richard Hofstadter's *Social Darwinism in American Thought*. *Journal of Economic Behavior & Organization* 71: 37–51.

London, J. [1903]1990. *The Call of the Wild*. New York: Dover.

Maine, H. J. S. 1861. *Ancient Law; Its Connection to the Early History of Society, and Its Relation to Modern Ideas*. London: John Murray.

Mill, J. S. 1859 [1993]. *On Liberty and Utilitarianism*. New York: Bantam.

1863[2008]. Utilitarianism. J.Bennett http://www.earlymoderntexts.com/assets/pdfs/mill1863.pdf.

Moore, G. E. 1903. *Principia Ethica*. Cambridge: Cambridge University Press.

Moore, J. R. 1986. "Socializing Darwinism": Historiography and the Fortunes of a Phrase. *Science as Politics*. Editor L. Levidow. London: Free Association Books.

Myers, F. W. H. 1881. George Eliot. *The Century Magazine*, November.

Nietzsche, F. 1895 [1920]. *The Anti-Christ*. Translator H. L. Menken. New York: Knopf.

1954. Twilight of the Idols. *The Portable Nietzsche*. Editor and translator W. Kaufmann. New York: Viking Press.

1966. *Beyond Good and Evil*. Translator W. Kaufmann. New York: Vintage Books.

1983. *Untimely Meditations*. Translator R. J. Hollingdale. Cambridge: Cambridge University Press.

1997. *Daybreak: Thoughts on the Prejudices of Morality. Translator R.J. Hollingdale*. Editors M. Clark, and B. Leiter. Cambridge: Cambridge University Press.

1998. *On the Genealogy of Morality*. Translators M. Clark, and A. Swensen. Indianapolis: Hackett.

2001. *The Gay Science*. Translator J. Nauckhoff. Cambridge: Cambridge University Press.

2006. *Thus Spoke Zarathustra. Translator A. Del Caro*. Editors A. Del Caro, and R. Pippen. Cambridge: Cambridge University Press.

Pence, C. H. 2011. Nietzsche's aesthetic critique of Darwin. *History and Philosophy of the Life Sciences* 33, no. 2: 165–90.

Pennock, R. 1998. *Tower of Babel: Scientific Evidence and the New Creationism*. Cambridge, Mass.: M.I.T. Press.

Radick, G. 2018. Darwinism and Social Darwinism. *The Cambridge History of Modern European Thought*. Editors Warren Breckman and Peter E. Gordon. Cambridge: Cambridge University Press.

Rawls, J. 1971. *A Theory of Justice*. Cambridge, Mass. Harvard University Press.

1980. Kantian constructivism in moral theory. *Journal of Philosophy* 77: 515–72.

Richards, R. J. 1987. *Darwin and the Emergence of Evolutionary Theories of Mind and Behavior*. Chicago: University of Chicago Press.

1992. *The Meaning of Evolution: The Morphological Construction and Ideological Reconstruction of Darwin's Theory*. Chicago: University of Chicago Press.

2008. *The Tragic Sense of Life: Ernst Haeckel and the Struggle over Evolutionary Thought*. Chicago: University of Chicago Press.

2013. *Was Hitler a Darwinian? Disputed Questions in the History of Evolutionary Theory*. Chicago: University of Chicago Press.

Richards, R. J., and M. Ruse. 2016. *Debating Darwin*. Chicago: University of Chicago Press.

Richardson, J. 2004. *Nietzsche's New Darwinism*. Oxford: Oxford University Press.

Roosevelt, T. 1899. The Strenuous Life. *Works*. Vol. XV, 267–81.

Ruse, M. 1979 a. *The Darwinian Revolution: Science Red in Tooth and Claw*. Chicago: University of Chicago Press.

1979b. *Sociobiology: Sense or Nonsense?* Dordrecht, Holland: Reidel.

1980. Charles Darwin and group selection. *Annals of Science* 37: 615–30.

1986a. *Taking Darwin Seriously: A Naturalistic Approach to Philosophy*. Oxford: Blackwell.

1986b. Evolutionary ethics: a phoenix arisen. *Zygon* 21: 95–112.

Editor. 1988 a. *But is it Science? The Philosophical Question in the Creation/ Evolution Controversy*. Buffalo, N.Y.: Prometheus.

1988b. *Homosexuality: A Philosophical Inquiry*. Oxford: Blackwell.

1996. *Monad to Man: The Concept of Progress in Evolutionary Biology*. Cambridge, Mass.: Harvard University Press.

2005. *The Evolution-Creation Struggle*. Cambridge, Mass.: Harvard University Press.

2013. *The Gaia Hypothesis: Science on a Pagan Planet*. Chicago: University of Chicago Press.

2015. *Atheism: What Everyone Needs to Know*. Oxford: Oxford University Press.

2017a. *Darwinism as Religion: What Literature Tells Us About Evolution*. Oxford: Oxford University Press.

2017b. *On Purpose*. Princeton, N. J.: Princeton University Press.

2017c. A Darwinian pilgrim's early progress. *Journal of Cognitive Historiography* 4, no. 151–164.

2017d. A Darwin's pilgrim's middle progress. *Journal of Cognitive Historiography, 2019*. 4, no. 165–179.

2017e. A Darwinian pilgrim's late progress. *Journal of Cognitive Historiography* 4: 180–198.

2018. *The Problem of War: Darwinism, Christianity, and Their Battle to Understand Human Conflict*. Oxford: Oxford University Press.

2019. *A Meaning to Life*. Oxford: Oxford University Press.

2021. *A Philosopher Looks at Human Beings*. Cambridge: Cambridge University Press.

Ruse, M., and R. J. Richards, Editors. 2017. *The Cambridge Handbook of Evolutionary Ethics*. Cambridge: Cambridge University Press.

Segerstrale, U. 1986. Colleagues in conflict: An in vitro analysis of the sociobiology debate. *Biology and Philosophy* 1: 53–88.

Shermer, M. 2002. *In Darwin's Shadow: The Life and Science of Alfred Russel Wallace*. New York: Oxford University Press.

Sidgwick, H. 1876. The theory of evolution in its application to practice. *Mind* 1: 52–67.

Sinclair, U. [1906] 2001. *The Jungle*. New York: Dover.

Spencer, H. 1851. *Social Statics: Or, the Conditions Essential to Human Happiness Specified, and the First of Them Developed*. London: Chapman.

1852a. A theory of population, deduced from the general law of animal fertility. *Westminster Review* ns. 1: 468–501.

1852b [1868]. The development hypothesis. *The Leader. Reprinted in Essays: Scientific, Political and Speculative*. H. Spencer, 377–83. London: Williams and Norgate.

1857 [1868]. Progress: Its law and cause. *Westminster Review* LXVII: 244–67.

1860. The social organism. *Westminster Review* LXXIII: 90–121.

1864. *Principles of Biology*. London: Williams and Norgate.

1879. *The Data of Ethics*. London: Williams and Norgate.

1882. *Political Institutions: Being Part V of the Principles of Sociology*. London: Williams and Norgate.

1892. *The Principles of Ethics*. London: Williams and Norgate.

Stitch, S. 1978. The recombinant DNA debate. *Philosophy and Public Affairs* 7: 187–205.

Strauss, D. F. 1835 [1892]. *The Life of Jesus Critically Examined.* Translator G. Eliot, New York: Macmillan.

1872. *The Old Faith and the New.* Translator M. Blind. Buffalo, N. Y.: Prometheus.

Sumner, W. G. 1914. *The Challenge of Facts: and Other Essays.* New Haven: Yale University Press.

Tennyson, A. 1850. *In Memoriam.* London: Edward Moxon.

Todes, D. P. 1989. *Darwin Without Malthus: The Struggle for Existence in Russian Evolutionary Thought.* New York, N.Y.: Oxford University Press.

Trivers, R L. 1971. The evolution of reciprocal altruism. *Quarterly Review of Biology* 46: 35–57.

Von Bernhardi, F. 1912. *Germany and the Next War.* London: Edward Arnold.

1914. *Britain as Germany's Vassal.* London: Dawson.

1920. *Vom Kriege der Zukunft. Nach den Erfahrungen des Weltkrieges.* Berlin: Mittler.

Wallace, A. R. 1858. On the tendency of varieties to depart indefinitely from the original type. *Journal of the Proceedings of the Linnean Society, Zoology* 3: 53–62.

1864. The origin of human races and the antiquity of man deduced from the theory of natural selection. *Journal of the Anthropological Society of London* 2: clvii-clxxxvii.

1899. The causes of war, and the remedies. *Clarion July* 18: 213.

1905. *My Life: A Record of Events and Opinions.* London: Chapman and Hall.

Weikart, R. 2004. *From Darwin to Hitler: Evolutionary Ethics, Eugenics, and Racism in Germany.* New York: Palgrave Macmillan.

Wells, H. G. [1895] 2005. *The Time Machine.* London: Penguin.

Wheeler, W. M. 1910. *Ants: Their Structure, Development and Behavior.* New York: Columbia University Press.

Whewell, W. 1840. *The Philosophy of the Inductive Sciences.* London: Parker.

Wilson, D. S., and Wilson E. O. 2007. Rethinking the theoretical foundation of sociobiology. *Quarterly Review of Biology* 82: 327–48

Wilson, E. O. 1975. *Sociobiology: The New Synthesis.* Cambridge, Mass.: Harvard University Press.

1984. *Biophilia.* Cambridge, Mass.: Harvard University Press.

1992. *The Diversity of Life.* Cambridge, Mass.: Harvard University Press.

1994. *Naturalist.* Washington, D.C.: Island Books/Shearwater Books.

2002. *The Future of Life.* New York: Vintage Books.

2006. *The Creation: A Meeting of Science and Religion.* New York: Norton.

2012. *The Social Conquest of Earth.* New York: Norton.

Cambridge Elements ≡

Elements in the Philosophy of Biology

Grant Ramsey
KU Leuven

Grant Ramsey is a BOFZAP research professor at the Institute of Philosophy, KU Leuven, Belgium. His work centers on philosophical problems at the foundation of evolutionary biology. He has been awarded the Popper Prize twice for his work in this area. He also publishes in the philosophy of animal behavior, human nature and the moral emotions. He runs the Ramsey Lab (theramseylab.org), a highly collaborative research group focused on issues in the philosophy of the life sciences.

Michael Ruse
Florida State University

Michael Ruse is the Lucyle T. Werkmeister Professor of Philosophy and the Director of the Program in the History and Philosophy of Science at Florida State University. He is Professor Emeritus at the University of Guelph, in Ontario, Canada. He is a former Guggenheim fellow and Gifford lecturer. He is the author or editor of over sixty books, most recently *Darwinism as Religion: What Literature Tells Us about Evolution; On Purpose; The Problem of War: Darwinism, Christianity, and their Battle to Understand Human Conflict;* and *A Meaning to Life.*

About the Series

This Cambridge Elements series provides concise and structured introductions to all of the central topics in the philosophy of biology. Contributors to the series are cutting-edge researchers who offer balanced, comprehensive coverage of multiple perspectives, while also developing new ideas and arguments from a unique viewpoint.

Cambridge Elements $\equiv$

Philosophy of Biology

Printed in the United States
by Baker & Taylor Publisher Services